THE ISLAND SUNRISE

𒊹𒊹𒊹𒊹𒊹𒊹

Jill Paton Walsh

All human achievement depends on a food surplus—only when a hunter could provide more
than enough food for his own needs could
others concentrate on toolmaking, carving, or
even painting.

During the vast period of time covered by
this book, man developed from a primitive,
restless, ape-like creature to a dweller in settled
communities, capable of husbanding his
resources and organising sustained corporate
effort. The Stone Age hunters made beautiful
and highly effective flint weapons. The farming
communities of the Neolithic period developed
the axes they needed for clearing the land, but
they also decorated them. In the Bronze and
Iron Ages, man found sufficient time and prosperity to offer patronage to craftsmen, priests,
and poets.

In her introduction to the book Jill Paton
Walsh defines 'culture' in terms of early man's
life as 'the traditional knowledge and behaviour
by which a people live and find their food; in
short, their way of life . . . a food surplus was
the first cultural triumph of mankind, upon
which all the rest has been built.'

Focusing her attention on prehistoric Britain,
Mrs. Walsh demonstrates her admiration for
these early peoples, ending each chapter with a
clear look forward that shows how much is
owed to the countless generations who first
inhabited the British Isles.

The book has seventy-one black-and-white
illustrations in the text and eight pages of full
colour.

🔲🔲🔲🔲🔲🔲

THE ISLAND SUNRISE

🔲🔲🔲🔲🔲🔲

THE ISLAND SUNRISE

🖾🖾🖾🖾🖾

PREHISTORIC CULTURE IN THE BRITISH ISLES

🖾🖾🖾🖾🖾

Jill Paton Walsh

A CLARION BOOK

The Seabury Press · New York

Library of Congress Cataloging in Publication Data

Walsh, Jill Paton, 1937–
   The island sunrise.

   "A Clarion book."
   Bibliography
   Includes index.
   SUMMARY: Describes the simple and useful artifacts
developed by prehistoric man which led to the production of a food surplus—the first cultural triumph of
mankind that made possible the further development
of civilization.
   1. Man, Prehistoric—Great Britain—Juvenile literature. 2. Great Britain—Antiquities—Juvenile lit-
ture.
   1. Man, Prehistoric—Great Britain. 2. Great
Britain—Antiquities. 1. Title.
GN805.W28 1976   936.2   75-4666
ISBN 0-8164-3155-8

Printed in Great Britain

for my daughter Clare, who likes to know

᠍᠍᠍᠍᠍᠍

ACKNOWLEDGEMENTS

᠍᠍᠍᠍᠍᠍

Acknowledgements are due to the following for permission to reproduce the colour and black and white plates:

Aerofilms Limited, 37, 38, 71; Ashmolean Museum, Oxford, 6, 35, 61; The British Broadcasting Corporation, 55; The British Library Board, 1; The Trustees of the British Museum, 9, *11*, *12*, *14*, *15*, 12, 13, 18, 25, 31, 43, 44, 53, 54, 58, 65, 66; The Trustees of the British Museum (Natural History), 2, 4; Brockhampton Press, Leicester, from *Buildings of Ancient Man* by H. and R. Leacroft, 62; Caisse Nationale des Monuments Historics, *1*; Cambridge University Collection, 22, 60; Faculty of Archaeology and Anthropology, Cambridge, *3*, 67; Cambridge University Press, from *Background to Archaeology* by D. Collins, R. Whitehouse, M. Henig and D. Whitehouse, 20; Colchester and Essex Museum, *13*; Ruth Crossley-Holland, 14; Danish National Museum, 2; Department of the Environment, Crown Copyright, 24, 27, 28, 29, 32, 33, 40, 70; Faber and Faber, London, from *Southern England: An Archaeological Guide* by James Dyer, 56; Hamish Hamilton, London, from *Stonehenge* by R. J. Atkinson, 41, 42; The Hermitage Museum, Leningrad, 10b; Hutchinson, London, from *Archaeology by Experiment* by M. L. Ryder, 21; Hutchinson, London, from *Prehistoric Societies* by Grahame Clarke and Stuart Piggott, 7, 8 15, 16, 17; Jean-Dominique Lajoux, 19; The London Museum, 57; Malcolm Murray, 69; Merseyside County Museums, Liverpool, 59; Musée des Antiquités Nationales, Château de St Germaine-en-Laye, 9; John Nance, Magnum Photos, 7; National Museum of Antiquities of Scotland, 6, 30, 46, 47, 50, 51; Naturhistorichen Museum, Vienna, 10a, 52; The Norfolk Museums Service, 25; Professor O'Kelly, University of Cork, *5*, *6*; Ordnance Survey Aerial Photography, Crown Copyright, 63; Pitt Rivers Museum, Oxford, 23, 36; Radio Times Hulton Picture Library, 34, 72; Reading Museum and Art Gallery, 45; The Royal Pavilion Art Gallery and Museums, Brighton, *10*; Thames and Hudson, London, from *The Stone Age Hunters* by Grahame Clarke, 19a; Stanley Thomas, 3, 5, 11, 39, 49, 64, 68; Wiltshire Archaeological Society Catalogue, 48; Wiltshire Archaeological and Natural History Society, *8*; and also to Jonathan Cape, London, for permission to reproduce the table 'Basic elements of the new chronology' from *Before Civilisation: the Radiocarbon Revolution and Prehistoric Europe* by Colin Renfrew.

🔁🔁🔁🔁🔁

CONTENTS

🔁🔁🔁🔁🔁

༒༒༒༒༒༒

INTRODUCTION

༒༒༒༒༒༒

THIS book is a cultural history of the British Isles in prehistoric times – that is until the Roman invasion of 55 BC. The cultural history of later times would deal with some of the most exalted achievements of mankind – books, paintings, sculpture and poems, things which have no 'use' except the delight which they give.

But in the beginning life was very simple. Mankind is a tribe of animals; to live we must eat, every day, or nearly every day. The remote ancestors of mankind lived by hand and eye; they found food like roots and berries, or they hunted and killed other animals for meat. In times and places when finding a day's food took all day nothing could be made, for a man or a woman who makes things – tools or clothes or cooking-pots, also needs to eat. People can make things instead of hunting only if those who hunt have more than enough for their own needs, have some to spare to feed the toolmakers and potters. When there is food to spare, then someone can have some time free for something other than hunting or gathering.

All the achievements of mankind are based on a food surplus, and that is as true today as it was half a million years ago. I can sit here, writing this book for you, only because someone else has planted, grown and harvested crops, reared animals for milk and meat, grown vegetables, and delivered all this food to shops near my home. If they had not, I should have no time to write about the past, or to think and find out about it, I would be scavenging for my supper. I would be hungry, and the food-quest would dominate my mind, blocking out thoughts of the past, or of the future beyond the next meal.

In this precarious state, driven by necessity, all mankind lived for vast stretches of time, and some do still in impoverished and remote places on the earth.

When we talk about the culture of early man we do not mean things like poetry and sculpture; the word has another, simpler meaning. It means the traditional knowledge and behaviour by which a people live and find their food; in short, their way of life. In this sense, all people, however primitive, have a culture. The cultures of early mankind did not include 'The fine arts'; for the first slender food surpluses and brief moments of spare time were devoted to the making of necessary things, things with a very immediate use, directly connected with eating – tools for the hunt and the butchering of meat.

This book will have much to say about very simple and useful artifacts, and will tell you about few things made only for delight; that is because a food surplus was the first cultural triumph of mankind, upon which all the rest has been built.

🖾🖾🖾🖾🖾

TRIBES OF WANDERERS

🖾🖾🖾🖾🖾

THE ground on which we stand, the rivers and valleys, the shape of the hill that rises nearest our home, and the familiar outline on maps of the shorelines of the continents and islands of the world seem solid and eternal, unchanging through countless ages. 'As old as the hills' we say, but even the hills had a birth, a beginning. It is only the pitiful shortness of human lives, lasting some hundred years at the most, that makes us think of the land as immobile. Just as a butterfly that lives for only a day can have no idea of the alternation of darkness and light, so we do not experience the ceaseless movement and change of the earth's surface. But sometimes the earth's crust breaks, and great floods of the molten lava beneath force their way through, or the drifting continents collide, and new mountains are thrust upwards, and all the while wind, frost and rain are at work eroding the hills, carrying down particles from the heights, to build up on the valley floors as fine-grained sediments that will later harden into new rocks. But the last great upheaval happened very long ago; only the occasional earthquake or suddenly erupting volcano remind us from time to time that even rock changes, even the hills come and go like the cloud formations above us, only more slowly.

Britain has not always been an island; indeed on the time-scale of the rocks it has not been an island very long. It was after the final cold period of the last Ice Age, one of the results of the great thaw, that the sea flooded the marshy estuary plain formed where the Thames and Rhine together ran northwards to the sea,

and made the North Sea. Then it broke through the line of chalk
hills to the Atlantic, making the English Channel, with the white
cliffs of Dover one side, facing the white cliffs of Calais on the
other.

At that time, around 8,000 years ago, mankind was already
old, but the rocks and soils of the British Isles were immeasur-
ably older. The rocks of the Outer Hebrides, for instance, and
parts of the Highlands of Scotland were created between 1,600
and 2,600 million years ago; the larger part of the Highlands
followed before 1,100 million years ago. The sandstones and
shales of Cornwall, south Wales, southern Ireland, and the
Orkneys were made some 350 million years ago, and so on, till
we reach the recent limestones of gentle hills like the Cotswolds,
which were made on ocean floors only 185 to 135 million years
ago, and the chalk hills, nearly new, some 70 million years old.

The rocks that were later to be Britain have lain under name-
less oceans, have been divided from Europe, and joined to North
America, have been hot like the hottest tropics, and have been
covered with ice like the Poles. In those distant times exotic
animals walked our rocks; Iguanodon left his footprints in the
Kentish Weald, fossil rhinoceros has been found at Ilford, fossil
mammoth at Aveley in Essex, while in Ireland giant deer are
found – their fossil skeletons large as horses, and their antlers
12 feet across the span.

By contrast with the rocks even the oldest ancestors of mankind
are only 25 million years old. But it was not in Britain, nor in
north-west Europe that the first creatures which can be called
man emerged. The cradle of humanity appears to have been
Africa. As far as we can tell, none of the great discoveries of the
Old Stone Age, the first epoch of prehistory, was made in the
British Isles, even the discovery of things which were necessary
for life here. In Africa starting some 2 million years ago, men
learned to make stone tools, and to hunt. These hunting creatures
spread very gradually, into Asia and Europe. The rate of change
was almost unimaginably slow. The first man-made tool, for
example, called a 'handaxe' by modern scholars, remained in
use, very little changed, for a quarter of a million years (see

plate 3). Nevertheless, during those slow centuries, people learned to control and kindle fire, to make clothes, to build shelters, and to speak to each other. Of all that we know very little. All that is left for us to study are bones, and the one durable thing the earliest people made – stone tools. That does not, of course, mean that they made nothing else – a good reminder of that is the wooden spear end from Clacton, one of the oldest British sites known to us, preserved by chance in peaty soil (see plate 1).

While the earliest toolmaking people were emerging and spreading across the continents of the Old World, Europe was in the grip of the Ice Age. The Ice Age was not just one 'glacial' or very cold period; it came and went, the climate changing and the ice retreating and advancing over and over again. At its farthest extent the ice-sheet covered the whole of Britain, down to the Thames, and the few remaining areas must have been desolate, bleak and cold, with at best the sort of vegetation called 'tundra' that in our time covers regions near the Pole – Lapland for example. But somewhere around 250,000 BC the climate warmed up, and an 'interglacial' or time of warmth between two glaciations began; this one was the second, or great interglacial because it lasted longer than the others. The ice retreated, and the first human colonists of the British Isles arrived.

Britain was still joined to the European continent, and yet the continuous influence that its geography has had on its history was already apparent, for these earliest occupants of Britain brought with them not one but two distinct 'cultures' – that is, two different ways of making stone tools. The first arrivals, called 'Clactonian' from Clacton in Essex, where their remains were first discovered, made their tools from flakes – that is from fairly flat plain pieces, knocked off a lump, or core of flint, and sometimes trimmed a little (see plate 2). This tradition seems to have come from the north European plain, that stretches all the way to Russia. Britain was, and is, at the western end of this great plain, the natural terminus of westward journeys.

In the same interglacial Britain was also inhabited by men using handaxes. These are made, not from the detached flakes, but from the central core of a piece of flint, chipped into the desired

1. Wooden spear and flint spokeshave
from Palaeolithic deposit, Clacton
on Sea, Essex.

shape by knocking waste pieces off both sides. This tradition is
the earliest toolmaking tradition. It spread from Africa to Europe,
along the shores and up the river valleys of the Mediterranean
and the Atlantic. Britain is the natural terminus of a north-
westerly coastal journey of this kind. The handaxes of these later
peoples are found widely in the British Isles, as far west as the
border with Wales, as far north as Yorkshire. The oldest handaxes found here are well made, and advanced in technique. They
have an attractive shape, and a rippled surface, like the sea (see
plate 3). The people who made them must have been hunters,
roving the land in small bands in search of game.

At one famous site – Swanscombe gravel pit in north Kent – a
large number of these fine tools were discovered, together with
part of the fossilized human skull of a young woman. This skull

2. Clactonian flake tools. Reading left to right: end scraper, butt-end
scraper, crescent scraper, side scraper, end scraper, bill-hook scraper,
pointed flake-tools ('hand-points').

is important in the difficult science of piecing together the evolution of the human body; in modern classifications it is the first from anywhere in the world to be counted as *Homo sapiens*, the surviving species. The gravel in which the Swanscombe woman was found also contained animal bones. Living at the same time as the owner of the skull had been straight-tusked elephants, rhinoceros, cave-bears, lions, horses, deer, giant ox, wolf and hare. Doubtless the Swanscombe people lived by hunting this game (see plate 4).

Perhaps the earlier Clactonians, whose typical flake-tools were found at Swanscombe in levels below the handaxes, and are therefore older, also lived by hunting large game. But the forests of their time offered plenty of other food – nuts and root plants, fishes from the rivers, birds and small woodland animals.

We know very little about the dwellings of these first inhabitants of Britain. Probably they made wind-breaks out of poles and branches. But at Stoke Newington in the nineteenth century a living area was found – two pointed stakes of birch, 4 feet long, which had supported branches of Clematis matted with fern. Many burnt stones tell us that the owners of this flimsy shelter had fires as well as a wind-break to ward off the cold.

3. The Swanscombe skull, and handaxes found with it.

4. Artist's impression of Swanscombe man hunting.

Since the flake-tool makers and the handaxe makers both lived
in Britain at the same time it is no surprise they met, and learned
from each other; towards the end of the interglacial a group of
people living near High Lodge in Suffolk made both kinds of tool.
As was to happen so often later, the British Isles, receiving in-
fluences from different sources, made of them a unique local
blend.

But the long warm interglacial came to an end, and the ice
advanced across northern Europe once more. As the climate got
harsher and colder in Europe a new way of making tools emerged,
perhaps growing out of a mixed tradition like the one at High
Lodge. This new technique used a core of flint very carefully
trimmed and prepared, so that with one final blow a large flake
could be struck off it that was a complete finished tool, needing
no more work. Such specially prepared cores are called 'tortoise-
cores' because of their humped shape (see plate 5).

This clever method was a quick way of producing a large, flat sharp edged flake-tool, with a shape and size rather like a thin oval handaxe. But often only one such tool could be struck from a single tortoise-core, so it was wasteful of flint. In southern England and northern France, however, where there was a plentiful supply of large flint nodules from the chalk hills the method flourished, and continued in use through the cold period of which we are speaking, and the next, and last interglacial, and into the final glacial of the Ice Age. Since flake-tools, as we saw earlier, come from more northerly places than the handaxe tradition, and since flakes are specially useful for skinning meat and preparing animal hides, perhaps it was in response to the increasing cold that the tortoise-core tools were developed.

5. Tortoise-core flake tools; a carefully prefabricated core, some 5 inches long for striking flakes of prepared shape like those in the foreground.

During the last interglacial, and the early part of the last advance of the ice-sheets, there appeared all over Europe south of the ice, and in the Middle East and North Africa, a culture called Mousterian (because it was first identified at Le Moustier in France) – a culture making very precise and neat tools, scrapers and handaxes of rather squat form. These tools are found with the bones of Neanderthal man – people of ape-like appearance, slightly stooped posture, and heavy bony ridges on their brows. The Neanderthalers are the people who most nearly resemble the popular idea of 'cave-men'. They did indeed take shelter from the severe cold by living in caves. On the cave floors the rubbish from their daily lives accumulated, and lay undisturbed. Because this rubbish is much easier to find than the debris lying on the open dwelling sites of earlier people, we know rather more about the Neanderthalers than their predecessors. They looked very primitive and savage, and doubtless in some ways they were. Not even one pierced tooth or bead has been found, to show that they adorned themselves, for example. And yet these people were the first, as far as we know, to have buried their dead. Neanderthal bones are found gently flexed, as though lying on their sides, and some of the bodies had been buried with ceremony of some kind. A child buried in Uzbekistan in central Asia, for example, was closely surrounded by a ring of goats' horns, pushed points downwards into the floor. A man found in the Zagros mountains in Iraq had apparently been laid on a thick bed of wild flowers, for pollen from flowers like grape hyacinth, bachelors buttons, hollyhocks and groundsel was found with his bones. The impression that a reverence for the dead implies some sort of respect for, and interest in, individual men instead of just the hunting tribe, is borne out by the Zagros burial. For the man buried there, apparently killed in a rock-fall, was an arthritic, one-armed cripple, and yet had reached an age of about forty. This man could never have taken a useful part in the hunt – his shoulder was undeveloped, and his arm had been amputated below the elbow. He must have been cared for, and fed, therefore, by others stronger than himself.

If the life-span of the one-armed man bears witness to the brotherly concern of his fellows, there are signs of other beliefs of the Neanderthalers that seem less pleasant to our way of thinking. Thus many skulls have been opened after death, as though to eat the brains, perhaps to transfer the strength and knowledge of the dead to the living.

The British Isles were barely habitable during the last great glaciation. The only Neanderthal bones found in Britain are on Jersey. Mousterian tools are found in small numbers in a handful of caves – probably Britain was never 'inhabited' by men of Neanderthal stock, but merely visited from time to time in milder phases of the Ice Age.

It is still a matter of debate among scholars what became of the Neanderthalers. We know that they were superseded, fairly abruptly, by men of modern type, with different traditions. This change was 'abrupt' compared to the extreme slowness of any previous change, though it took longer than the time which has elapsed between the earliest cities of Egypt and the present day. Some people think the Neanderthalers were our ancestors in a direct line – that they evolved into modern man, though the time seems short for so great an evolutionary change. Others think that modern man and the Neanderthalers confronted each other – even fought – and the Neanderthalers with their lower intelligence and less-developed culture lost, leaving modern man to inherit the earth. Yet the earth is large, and men of any type were very few; surely some pockets of Neanderthalers should have survived. Besides there is no clear evidence of modern man emerging at the same time as Neanderthal man in any major region of the world. At the present state of knowledge the question has to be left open.

Whatever the reason may have been, we do know that in western Europe the Mousterian culture which belonged to the Neanderthalers disappears on the arrival of 'Cromagnon' men – men of modern type, during a milder phase of the final glaciation, around 40,000 to 29,000 BC. The newcomers, from whom we are all descended, brought the art of working stone into tools to a new peak of refinement. Their tools, in a great variety of shapes for many different special needs were made from 'blades' rather than from 'flakes'. A blade is a very long, straight-sided flat flake, struck from a pre-prepared fluted core with great precision and skill (see plate 6). Such slender sharp blades of flint could be made into tools of beauty and efficiency; the working of flint reached such proficiency that even the invention of bronze did

6. The last refinement of toolmaking in flint; 'blades' struck from prepared core. From Ertebolle, Denmark.

not displace flint; flint was to continue in use for a long time beside bronze, even imitating forms natural to metal.

With the arrival in western Europe of this new, highly inventive human strain a new situation arose. Always before, so slow was the pace of any change in human culture, that although ideas and methods spread extremely gradually, they spread to the entire population before being overtaken by some further change. But now the speed of change increased, so that diffusion (that is the spread of ideas) could no longer keep up with it, and for the first time we find local cultures developing and changing in one region, while the rest of the human population lag behind. The region in which above all the new culture (called 'Upper Palaeolithic', that is late Old Stone Age) flourished was south-western France and northern Spain.

This region was rich in caves, often grouped closely enough to make of their inhabitants a society larger than a wandering hunting group could have been. The effect of the Ice Age was to displace southwards the climatic zones familiar to us at the present day, so that the Mediterranean region was covered with deciduous forest, merging with coniferous forest on higher ground. Farther north and eastwards in central Europe the land was covered with tundra – grasses and dwarf shrubs and trees. So much water was locked in vast ice-sheets that the sea level was some 100 metres lower than at the present time. Where the North Sea now is, dry land joined Britain to the European plains. On these open plains animals roamed – mammoth and woolly rhinoceros, and huge herds of reindeer, and in the more woodland areas wild ox and wild boar, while wild horse and bison which can live in either wood or grassland were abundant. On this plentiful game the advanced Palaeolithic hunters lived, rather as in modern times the North American Indian lived on the buffalo.

The abundance of game, and the tool- and weapon-making skill of the inhabitants of that region of south-western Europe produced a food surplus, which must at least sometimes have been a generous one, more than enough to make time for toolmaking. The toolmaking indeed flourished, and grew ever more elaborate and closely adapted to the particular job. Toolmaking traditions followed one after another in the caves of that region: Aurignacian, Gravettian, Solutrean and finally Magdalenian cultures are distinguished by scholars, each divided into early and late phases by the dozen.

To look very briefly and in broad outline at what happened

we can pick out three important changes. Firstly with the use of
flint blades a number of new tools appeared in the 'tool-kit'. A
long blade with one edge blunted like a penknife, for instance,
tanged and barbed points for spears, pointed tools for piercing,
and the burin – a chisel-like blade with a sharp squared-off end,
for splitting and engraving bone, or working wood. Secondly, as
the invention of the burin suggests there was a vastly increased
use of materials other than stone, especially bone. Starting with
simple points the bonework develops till in the Magdalenian
phase there are delicately made barbed harpoons, fine needles,
and spear throwers, rods and batons carved and decorated (see
plates 7, 8, 9). There were also composite tools, made from more
than one material – wood and flint, or wood and bone.

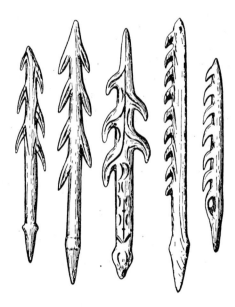

7. Advanced Palaeolithic (Magdalenian) harpoon-heads of reindeer antler.

Thirdly and most astonishing of all the food surplus was used
to create the first art. The Gravettian culture, for instance, produced many little statuettes called 'venuses', although the women

8. Magdalenian decorative art: spiral ornament on antler rods from Isturitz, Basses Pyrénées, France.

portrayed would not seem beautiful to modern eyes. It is clearly their sexual characteristics that are celebrated: they have huge breasts, bellies and buttocks and seem to be pregnant. Their heads, hands and feet are often sketchily indicated, and they have no faces (see plate 10). It seems obvious that they represent a concern with fertility. Beautiful or not they are forcefully expressive. Undeniably beautiful are the decorations applied to rods and spear-throwers, animal forms and elaborate spiral patterns (see plates 8, 9). And most spectacular of all is the painting of animal forms on the walls of caves. Wall-painting begins in the Aurignacian phase, gathers strength in the Solutrean, and flowers in the Magdalenian. An astonishing variety of techniques was used. Colour was applied to the walls of caves by finger-tracing, painting, rubbing on with 'crayons' of coloured rock, and blowing on in powder form; outlines were drawn, or engraved, or even deeply cut out to make a sculptured 'bas-relief'. But it is not only the techniques that deserve admiration. This is the first art of the world, and yet it can be compared with almost any achievement. You can look in vain for a later artist who surpasses the unknown prehistoric painters in conveying strength and movement, or for representations of animals who seem as essentially themselves as they do in red, or ochre, or brown on the walls of caves (see colour plate 1).

It has been common to define mankind as essentially tool-making. But whether or not we would think of the earliest tool-makers as human if we could be transported in time to meet

9. 'Batons de commandement' from Le Placard,
France, carved with animal heads.

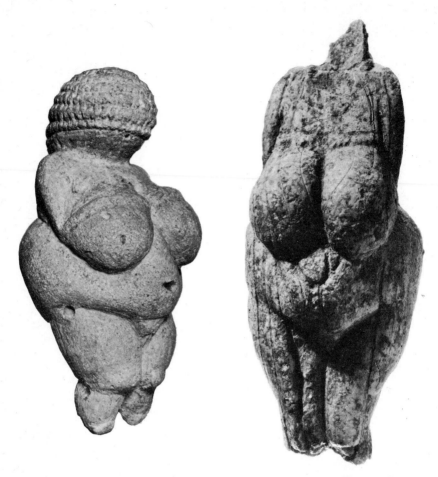

10. Palaeolithic statuettes: *a*. The 'Venus' of Willendorf.
b. Mammoth bone 'Venus' from Kostenki.

them, there is surely no doubt at all about the makers of cave painting. Experts give strange-sounding explanations of the purpose and intention of this art – it was hunting-magic, totemism, fertility magic, sympathetic magic: but whatever the artist was painting *for*, we can see from his work that he had eyes and hands like ours, vision like ours. Mankind is a tribe of image-makers, any image-maker is one of us.

While the first artists were working and flourishing in south-western Europe, Britain was bleak and desolate, covered with ice-sheet as far as the midlands, and affording very little warmth, and very little food, and only a few caves, widely scattered, to shelter in. Nevertheless, a few hardy folk braved the harsh conditions, and came here, bringing faint echoes of the cultures of southern France. Thus leaf-shaped points from the earliest phase of the Solutrean are found in Britain and in its few caves tools made from blades of flint. There is even a crudely engraved 'baton' from Gough's Cave in Cheddar Gorge, and from caves at Cresswell Crags in Derbyshire, two pieces of bone, one with a scratched horse's head, the other with an incised human figure, perhaps a masked dancer (see plates 11, 12, 13).

Very little happened in ice-bound Britain during the great age of cave painting, but things were happening elsewhere. The

11. Antler Batons from Gough's Cave, Cheddar.

12. Upper Palaeolithic engraving of a horse's head on a rib of bone, from Robin Hood's Cave, Cresswell Crags, Derbyshire.

spread of mankind over the face of the earth, impelled by the wanderings of the hunter, had led to the settlement of the American continent before the end of the final glaciation. Probably the crossing from Asia to Alaska took place during a milder phase of the Ice Age, but although evidence is very scant, we know that by 12,000 BC hunters using finely shaped flint points were flourishing on the high plains of North America.

13. Engraving of a stylized human figure, possibly a masked dancer from Pin Hole Cave, Cresswell Crags.

Spectacular though the achievements of the hunting and food-gathering cultures of France and Spain were, they were not able to survive the great climatic change which began about 8,000 B C. This change was the last retreat of the ice, leading to the warm phase in which we now live. The vast ice mass did not, of course, disappear all at once; it grew smaller year by year until, like a pond thawing, it was suddenly melted. The temperature rose; huge areas of land that had lain under the glaciers and ice-sheets were opened up. The sea-level rose rapidly as it accepted the floods of melt-water, and land levels that had been depressed by the sheer weight of ice resting on them slowly recovered. The warmer weather produced a dramatic change in the plant cover, the open tundra being grown over by forest, except on mountains and in marshes. First came a scatter of willow, birch and pine, then dense pine-forest, and finally, as the weather got still warmer, oak, elm, lime and alder, the familiar deciduous forest that still grows in patches even in Britain, intensively farmed and built up though it now is (see map, plate 14).

These changes sound to us like an improvement, but to the Late Palaeolithic hunters they were a disaster. The herds of cold-loving game animals on which they had lived died out, or moved away to the extreme north, the thickening forest protected the woodland animals and made hunting them more difficult, and cut off one encampment of people from another. The Azilian culture, which succeeds the Magdalenian in France is in all respects impoverished by comparison. The Azilians made smaller, finicky flints, fewer objects in antlery, and those less well worked. They lived in the painted caves, but made no more pictures on the walls, and all that remained to them of the carving and decorative art of their forebears were lines and dots painted on river-smoothed pebbles. The rich food surplus of the Ice Age had gone for good.

There was one very widespread change in toolmaking methods in response to these changes. The size of the points and blades made from flint became much smaller. Some of the new small points were made by snapping a long blade diagonally across into triangular or trapeze-shaped pieces. Such microliths (that is

Britain after the Ice Age

plate 14

little stones) were then mounted and slotted into wooden shafts, making spears, harpoons and arrows (see plate 15). These very different weapons reflect the new hunting conditions in forests – the need to take small game and birds, and the increasing use of bow and arrow rather than the older spear and spear thrower.

The forests obstructed the movements of groups of people; nevertheless at least one great movement of population took place – northwards into the huge low-lying north European plain, stretching from eastern England to Russia, which had formerly been covered with ice. As the forest spread, encampments concentrated on the river-margins, and the edges of the numerous lakes of melt-water. The peat which has gradually filled many of these lakes has preserved for us most of what we know about these northern people, and given them their name in archaeology – 'Maglemosians' from Danish words meaning 'great bog'.

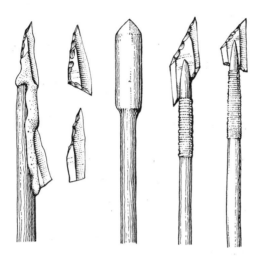

15. Mesolithic arrows set with flint microliths, and wooden bolt, from north-west Europe.

The Maglemosian northerners met the changed world with vigour and intelligence. Their culture clearly stems from that of the cave-artists, adapted to meet the new circumstances. The two most important new inventions were axes and boats, with which to cope with the forests and waters of the new climate. The axes were made from flint cores and sharpened by transverse blows like those for making burins. They were mounted in wooden handles, with antler sleeves to help absorb the impact of the blows. And they were surprisingly effective; modern experiments with ancient axe-heads in reconstructed new wooden handles, have shown that an area of 500 square metres could be cleared by three men in four hours work. As well as axes, adzes for working wood obtained by tree-felling appear in Maglemosian

times (see plate 16). The boats were dug-out tree trunks, pro-
pelled by wooden paddles. Wood was being used on a large scale;
the Maglemosians liked to live near water, and they made lakeside platforms out of felled trees for dwelling sites, and doubtless,
wooden huts too, about which we know very little, though in
Denmark some rectangular huts have been found, with tree-bark
floors, and walls of small branches bent and tied at the top to
form a roof.

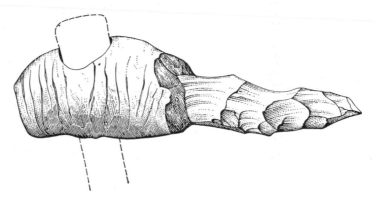

16. Maglemosian flint adze-head set in wooden holder, perforated for
handle, from the Elbe–Trave Canal, Schleswig-Holstein.

Like the Magdalenians of the earlier period the Maglemosians
made lavish use of antler and bone from animals killed in the
hunt. From these they made holders for axes and adzes, skin-
working tools, fish-hooks, netting needles, awls and barbed spearheads. Although they still lived mainly by hunting, they were
also exploiting the waters beside which they lived. As well as
boats they had fish-traps, and nets woven from bark fibre,
weighted by stones, and floated with bark floats. They liked ornaments, and made necklaces and pendants from amber, stone, and
pierced animal teeth. And although there were no caves to be
painted in northern Europe, they still carved small objects,
decorated surfaces with engraved lines and neatly drilled holes,
and made little animals from lumps of amber where it was
plentiful, round the Baltic shore (see colour plate 2).

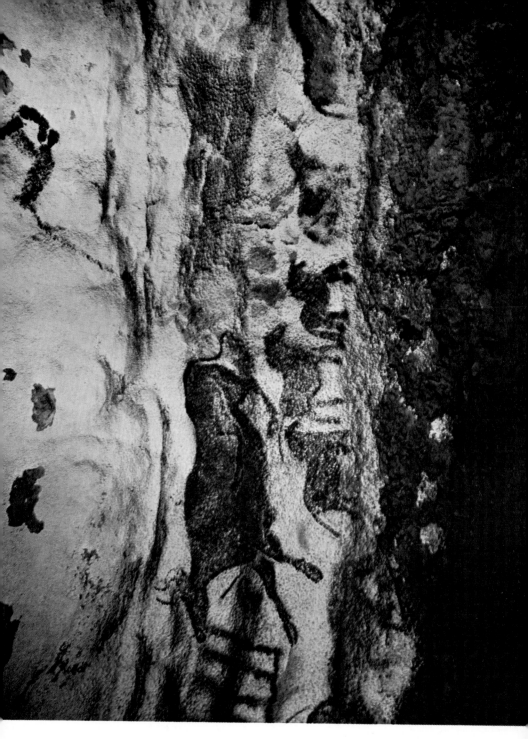

1. Palaeolithic wall-painting: Jumping Cow and Horses from Lascaux

2. Maglemose carvings from Denmark

5,6. Decorated megaliths from the grave at the New Grange in Ireland

We get a vivid picture of a Maglemosian encampment from the excavation at Star Carr in Yorkshire. Quite large trees, demonstrating the efficiency of the available axes, had been cut and laid down to make a lakeside dwelling platform. The axe marks on the trees can still clearly be seen. Found on the site was a good selection of flint and bone tools, and although there were no amber carvings, there was a charming necklace of shale and amber beads. There were a number of rolls of birch bark, perhaps used for making containers, like the little boxes of bark that are still made by some North American Indians, perhaps used to yield the resin with which microliths were stuck to arrow or spear shafts. A lump of iron pyrites was found – surely used with flint to strike sparks for kindling fire. The hunters of Star Carr had lived on elk, wild ox, red deer, roe deer, wild boar, fox, beaver and marten. Almost certainly, since a wooden paddle was found, they were fishermen too. The boat with which the paddle was used was not found, but was probably like the one from some thousand years later found at Pesse in Holland (see plate 17).

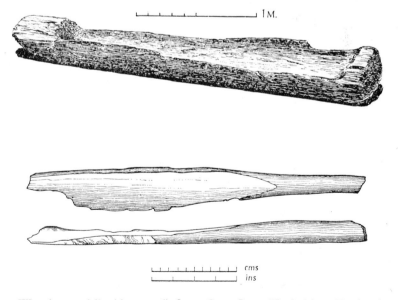

17. Wooden paddle (damaged) from Star Carr, Yorkshire, England. Dug-out boat from Pesse, Drenthe, north Holland.

The Star Carr folk kept a dog – the oldest known domesticated dog. Most interesting of all are the antler frontlets that were found here. These are a pair of head-dresses made from a stag's skull with the antlers left in place, but hollowed out, presumably to make them lighter to wear. They have been pierced for thongs to hold them on the head (see plate 18). These might have been worn with a deer-hide, as a disguise when tracking deer, or they might have been part of a ceremony of some kind. Either way they connect back in time to the famous masked dancer from the Trois Frères Cave in France (see plate 19), and forwards in time to the horned head-dresses worn by folk-dancers to within living memory in various places in England, and at Abbot's Bromley in Shropshire to the present day. Yet between Star Carr and the present lies a gulf of over 9,000 years.

The talented Maglemosians were not the only Mesolithic (that is middle Stone Age) inhabitants of Britain. There were also simpler, poorer people, making tiny flints to barb their arrows with, but using no axes, and practising no art, who wandered as hunters and fowlers in sandy places and along river-courses where the forest cover was thinner.

Meanwhile, the ice-cap continued to shrink and thaw, sea-levels rose, and flooded many of the lake-scattered forested areas in which the Maglemosians had lived. The North Sea came into being, the land bridge between western Scotland and northern Ireland was breached, and finally, somewhere around 6,000 BC the chalk ridge between Dover and Calais was washed away, and Britain became an island. That did not necessarily make it more remote. The forests and marshes of the North Sea plain cannot have been easy to travel through, and as we have seen simple boats were already in use. There is some evidence to suggest that Mesolithic folk were already seafarers.

Swept round by Atlantic waters Britain warmed up still further. Beech trees appeared in the southern forests, and shell-fish flourished on the coastline. In north-west Ireland and western Scotland a culture developed that was heavily dependent on shell-fish, and used a special flint pick for hacking molluscs off

18. *a.* ⎫
    b. ⎬ Antler frontlets from Star Carr, Yorkshire.

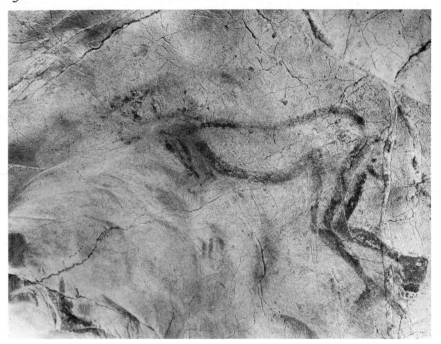

19. The 'Sorcerer'
from Les Trois Frères Cave, France,
wearing a horned head-dress.
a. The original.

b. A reconstructed drawing.

rocks. Similar groups of 'strand-loopers' (that is beach-dwellers) also lived on the Baltic coasts.

This simple way of life – hunting the available game, and gathering the available food with tools made of flint, bone, and wood continued for many centuries among the few inhabitants of Britain, until around 4,500 BC. But elsewhere the time of the hunter was over. For at about the same time as the people of Star Carr built their lakeside camp, at Jericho in the Middle East a 10-acre town was being fortified with stone walls, and towers 30 feet high. And the prosperous people of Jericho were using flint blades which have a peculiar lustrous sheen, which is known to be caused by using flint to cut the stalks of grasses. They had begun to harvest grain.

Afterthought

IT is only too easy looking back on the Stone Age, to think of the progress of mankind as a kind of staircase, of which we are at the top. The men and women whose tools and way of life we have been describing can easily seem to have been our inferiors, grossly simple compared to us, 'primitives', even 'savages'. Yet the cave-art of France and Spain ought alone to teach us that there is no connection between hunting and food-gathering as a means of supporting life and a lack of intellectual or spiritual qualities. The achievements of ancient hunters are worthy of our astonishment and respect. Travelling on foot, and with such simple tools and weapons as we have described, they had colonized the entire habitable surface of the earth, with the exception of the remotest Pacific islands. They invented cutting tools, clothing, houses, and the control of fire, and by stages of which we know nothing, and by a process we can only guess at, they discovered and acquired language and art.

Their way of life has not passed away, but is lived at the present moment in various forms and traditions in widely scattered places on the earth. In many of these places – the circumpolar lands of the Eskimo, the harsh deserts of the Kalahari and the Australian interior it is still the only possible life-style. The confrontation between modern man and surviving hunter food-gatherers which took place as modern men undertook the intensive exploration of the globe, and is still taking place today is almost always a severe shock to both sides. Even so wise and intelligent a man as Charles Darwin, seeing the seeming misery and squalor of the life of the Canoe Indians, could write 'Viewing such men one can hardly make oneself believe that they are fellow-creatures and inhabitants of the same world'. Other men, seeing the seemingly carefree life of men who 'did no work' but lived off the fruits of the land, were reminded of the Garden of Eden, and, like the philosopher Rousseau, idealized primitive man, attributing to him every moral virtue and inventing the idea of 'the noble savage'.

Idealized or despised, primitive peoples have almost everywhere fared very badly at the hands of more 'advanced' men. They have been exploited, enslaved, dispossessed and exterminated, and they have suffered all this at the hands of those who all the while considered themselves the superiors of their victims. The sorry story of the fate of the North American Indian is example enough, yet the destruction of 'natives' has not ceased, but continues to this day in South America among other places. '"Yes," said Chiparopai, an old Yuma Indian, "we know that when you come, we die."'*

Yet in extreme environments – dense jungle, blazing deserts, polar wastes, the boot is on the other foot, and primitives survive and support themselves without exhausting the slender resources of the land, in places where a modern man dies within days unless he can bring tons of modern equipment with him. Consider an Australian Aborigine family. Man and wife can carry all they own in their four hands. But scant though their possessions are, they have all they need to live. They have rights and duties in their kin and tribe, they have a religion, art, and a rich folk-lore. Like us they are the descendants of the ancient hunter food-gatherers. So closely does the way of life of modern hunter food-gatherers mirror the ancient, that it is often possible to illuminate

* Curtis: *The Indians Book.*

the meaning of archaeological finds by studying the present, or to find a tool made yesterday identical in form and function with one made 6,000 years ago. It is the staggering changes in *our* culture that make the distance between us and them, and produce such mind-boggling things as a colour photograph of a stone-age man making fire (see colour plate 3) or a spear-head made from a flaked core of bottle glass (colour plate 4).

As to whether the changes that have come about are for the better there can be more than one opinion about that. This, for example, is what Chief Flying Hawk, a Sioux Indian, had to say about houses:

> 'The tipi is much better to live in, always clean, warm in winter, cool in summer, easy to move. The white man builds big house, cost much money, like big cage, shut out sun, can never move, always sick. Indians and animals know better how to live than white man; nobody can be in good health if he does not have all the time fresh air, sunshine and good water. If the Great Spirit wanted men to stay in one place he would make the world stand still; but he made it always to change, so birds and animals can move and always have green grass and ripe berries, sunlight to work and play, and night to sleep; summer for flowers to bloom, and winter for them to sleep, always changing, everything for good, nothing for nothing.'*

Any wandering man, even the ancient hunters who roamed Britain when it was first an island, might have felt and thought like that.

It would be a mistake, too, to suppose that the only survivals from those remote times are among uncivilized people far away. The time is long past when hunting wild life in Britain could provide much food; yet men evolved over millions of years as hunters, and hunting is still returned to as a recreation by the privileged. Fox-hunting, stag-hunting, otter hunting, fly-fishing and shooting grouse still give pleasure to those who can afford them, and every water's edge in Britain that is not hopelessly polluted is frequented by fishermen. You yourself, perhaps, have

* M. I. McCrieght: *Firewater and Forked Tongues.*

experienced unreasonable delight at finding bilberries, black-berries, or cob-nuts there for the taking in the countryside, or in netting shrimps, or collecting cockles on the shore. And the nearest hunter food-gatherers to you are the captains and crews of the trawlers in your nearest fishing port.

If there is anything more remarkable than how much, in the last few thousand years, human beings have changed, it is how little.

🔯🔯🔯🔯🔯🔯

FIRST SETTLERS

🔯🔯🔯🔯🔯🔯

'FARMING' could only be discovered in places where the animals and cereal grasses of which it makes use were to be found roaming or growing wild. The wild varieties ancestral to wheat and barley are native to various parts of the Middle East, especially Asia Minor, Palestine, and eastwards towards the Zagros mountains. The wild ancestors of sheep and goats also lived in these regions, and so did wild cattle and wild pig, though these were more widespread, living in most of Europe and Asia except the far north, and in North Africa.

Not surprisingly then, the change from simply gathering cereal grains from wild grasses to sowing seed and harvesting, and the change from hunting animals to herding them took place in the Middle East.

These spectacular and far-reaching changes in the means of supporting life, together with the discovery of pottery, weaving, and the making of ground and polished stone axes used to be lumped together and called 'The Neolithic Revolution'. More recently it has been realized that this 'revolution' did not happen suddenly and all at once. The earliest reapers of grain were still Mesolithic, depending chiefly on hunting for their food; the earliest farming communities had not yet learned to make pottery, and farming itself, involving the control and exploitation of different animals and crops is not one but many inventions not necessarily connected, and happening in a different sequence in different areas. Thus on present evidence the domestication of animals came before the growing of crops in the Zagros mountains, while in Asia Minor and the Levant there were people growing crops who had no domestic animals as yet.

Of more direct importance to the story of Britain, however, is the way in which the multiple new inventions spread across Europe, and into the British Isles. Since the spread of farming involved the diffusion of plants and animals outside their original native areas, the idea could not spread by itself, and some movement of peoples must have been involved. As the farming economy moved farther away from its place of origin, it changed and adapted itself to local conditions and local flora and fauna. Millet was probably first grown in Greece, for example, and later spelt wheat, rye and oats became significant crops first in northern Europe.

There were three broad routes by which farming peoples spread across Europe (see plate 20). These were along the Danube and its tributaries; along the northern coast of the Mediterranean, through Greece, Italy, southern France, and Spain, with a branching movement into northern France, and thence to Britain; and across the north Europe plain. The traditions spreading up the Danube basin, though they reached Holland, did not cross the English Channel; the first farmers in Britain seem to have belonged to the 'western Neolithic' tradition that had spread by way of the Mediterranean coasts, with an admixture of people coming from the north European plain.

Whoever they were the first farmers in Britain must necessarily have been seafarers, and capable of bringing their seed corn and their animals with them. The dug-out boats which we know the Mesolithic hunters used seem scarcely good enough, even if the animals were brought as young lambs and calves. Perhaps a fair-weather crossing could be made on some kind of raft. The land they arrived at was thickly forested everywhere except where it was marshy; the newcomers set about clearing the trees from the less dense forests on the chalky uplands of which much of southern and eastern England consists.

Because the chalk and limestone hills are bare of trees at the present time, and have always been open grasslands as far back as we know for certain, it used to be thought that this had always

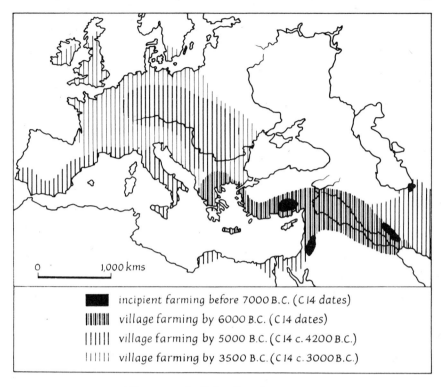

20. The spread of the farming economy.

been so, and that it was because of the openness of the region that the first farming settlements were made on the southern uplands. Two different kinds of archaeological research have recently changed this picture. Firstly the pollen that lies in the soil at different levels can be studied to discover exactly what the plant cover was at particular times. Pollen analysis at Hockham Mere, in East Anglia, for example, has shown that before the arrival of the first farmers the plants shedding pollen on the ground were oak, alder, elm, lime, and other plants characteristic of closed forest. During the Neolithic period a change took place. The amount of tree pollen lessens, suggesting that about a third of the trees in the surrounding district had been cleared by the end of Neolithic times. At the same time new kinds of pollen appeared – those of wild grasses, suggesting the growth of pasture;

those of weeds that tend to invade cleared land, like plantain, mugwort and goosefoot, and those of cereals, together suggesting arable farming, and finally those of the heather family, suggesting the growth of heath on abandoned fields.

Experiments with reconstructed ancient ploughs (see plate 21) have confirmed the new picture by showing that it is in fact not at all easy to plough 'open' country with the means available to Neolithic settlers; grass is hard to plough, because the share slides out of the turf in a yard or so. It may well be that the soft humus-laden forest floor was easier to bring into cultivation, in spite of the trees that had first to be cleared from it.

21. Reproduction of ancient plough in use. An archaeological experiment in Denmark.

What kind of people began the transformation of the British Isles from virgin forest to the 'field plotted and pieced, fold fallow and plough'* of the present day? In southern England farming was begun by people called after Windmill Hill in Wiltshire, where a settlement of theirs has been excavated. The Windmill Hill people kept cattle, pigs, sheep, goats and dogs; they culti-

* Gerard Manley Hopkins: *Pied Beauty*.

vated einkorn and emmer wheat, and a little barley, and grew flax, probably for the food value of its seeds, since no weaving equipment has been found. Wild apple seeds show that they also gathered available fruits. They made plain dark pottery, mainly round-bottomed, bag-shaped vessels, but also some with a burnished surface which was made within reach of Devon and Cornwall since it contains grit from rocks in the south-west. Animal husbandry was at least as important to these folk as field crops, for it led to the making of the first large structures in Britain – causewayed camps. These camps are large earthwork enclosures, often of more than one ring of ditches, the ditches being interrupted by several undug portions making bridges into the middle (see plate 22). The presence in these camps of large quantities of cattle bones showing signs of slaughtering, and of numerous flint scrapers used for cleaning hides, and antler combs for removing coarse hair from skins, gives us a clue to their probable purpose. Most likely they were for rounding up and sorting out cattle to

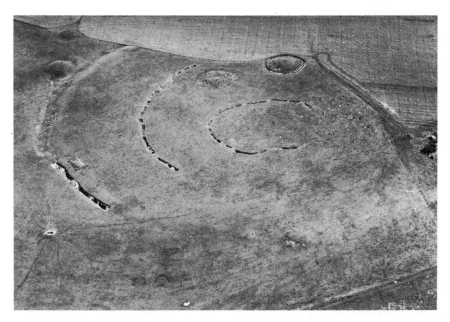

22. The 'causewayed camp' at Windmill Hill, Wiltshire.

be slaughtered in the autumn, since only in modern times has it become possible to feed large herds through the winter. We may imagine people gathering from their small fields scattered in woodland, camping in the causewayed camp, feasting on the slaughtered cattle, and making clothes for the winter from the supply of hides. There is no sign of permanent houses within the enclosures. Among the domestic refuse the campers left, however, are some slaughtered human bones, and some skulls pierced to extract the brains – it seems the Windmill Hill people were occasional cannibals. In their encampments and burials a few rough mother-goddess figurines have been found, and likewise chalk or bone representations of a phallus, which suggest that these people shared a fertility cult which was widespread on the continent, and among western Neolithic people generally, and which doubtless goes back to the fertility-cult of the ancient hunters.

There is a curious contrast between the butchered human bones mentioned above, or the body of a young girl thrown on the rubbish in the ditch of a causewayed camp at Whitehawk, Sussex, and the burial of other Neolithic dead in 'long barrows'. The long barrows are huge elongated mounds of earth raised over a temporary wooden structure in which several bodies were laid. Perhaps all the dead of a little settlement or a large family were collected in one of these structures before the barrow was built; once built it was sealed. Such large and impressive burial mounds must have taken the labour of many months and many hands to raise. At some there are traces of a funeral feast which rewarded the workers or mourners. Long barrows are a common sight all over the chalklands of southern England; it is worth pausing to notice that they are the oldest man-made things still visible to a casual eye in the landscape.

The need to clear forest for fields, and then, as the fields were exhausted, to clear virgin forest for more fields, produced a continuous need for one tool above all – for axes. Everywhere Neolithic cultures made use of an improved form of stone axe: after being chipped to shape in the old way, it was ground and polished, giving it a smooth surface (see plate 23). In Britain

23. Polished axe of Cumbrian origin, found near Bampton, Oxon.

the early farmers were supplied with axes from two sources, trading and mining, both of which show an advance in the organization of life. We know about the trade in axes because of axes made of other stone than flint, which appear all over the British Isles, widely scattered. These handsome ground and polished tools are of great interest, because their places of origin can be scientifically determined. The rocks from which they are made are the igneous rocks from remote western districts of Britain, from Land's End, the Prescelly mountains in Wales, the Lake District, and even northern Ireland. A glance at a map showing where Cornish axes have been found shows that they were widely distributed by trade routes along river valleys, and round the coasts. These first signs of the development of trading are of great interest, because without trading the simple farming communities could not advance towards the more specialized and less self-sufficient pattern of life that was on the way. But we should not imagine that trade meant merchants with a large stock-in-trade, spending their time travelling and hawking their wares. The movement of axes may represent a simpler form of barter, or the exchange of ceremonial gifts. This is made more likely by the obviously ritual or ceremonial form of some of the axes – fashioned from beautiful but soft stones, like sandstone, jade or jadeite. The exchange is clearly shown also by polished flint axes found in a recent excavation at Carn Brea in Cornwall, for flint is to be found only in eastern England.

In the east the superior veins of high-quality flint which lay deep in the chalk were obtained by mining. Using the same very primitive tools with which they had raised the long barrows, antler picks, and ox shoulder-blade shovels, Neolithic workers sank shafts down into the chalk, and galleries running along the flint seams, radiating from the foot of the shafts (see plate 24). The miners must have worked by lamplight – using hollowed chalk cups filled with grease and a wick. The flint was roughed out into axes ready for polishing immediately it was brought to the surface; at Grimes Graves in Norfolk, the best-known flint mine, the area round the mineshafts is covered with debris from flint knapping, to a depth of 5 feet in places. Some of the mines here have been excavated and one can be visited.

24. Grimes Graves, Norfolk. Foot of a mine shaft, with radiating galleries.

The Grimes Graves miners used pottery of Windmill Hill type, but it is quite likely that the idea of mining for flint reached England from across the North Sea, rather than originating here, for flint mines are also known in Belgium, Holland and northern

4. A spearhead flaked
from bottle-glass
by an Australian
Aborigine

A man of the Tasaday tribe makes fire

7. Carved stone balls, perhaps ceremonial mace heads, and found mainly in eastern Scotland and the northern isles

11. The Desborough Mirror; polished bronze, engraved in La Tene style

France, and also farther north in Denmark, Sweden and Poland. In any case, the Windmill Hill people were not the only inhabitants of Britain at that time.

In the first place there must still have been Mesolithic hunters, food-gathering folk wandering the forests. Indeed, there are a few aspects of Grimes Graves that suggest a link with the older way of life. The very large quantity of red deer antlers which were used as picks to shift the chalk in the mines proves that the miners either hunted themselves, or, much more likely, traded with hunters of deer; and there is a roughly scratched drawing of a deer on a crust of flint found at Grimes Graves, which, crude though it is, suggests the style of Mesolithic art (see plate 25). Moreover the most spectacular find at Grimes Graves was a 'shrine' – an arrangement at the foot of a pit where the flint had been exhausted, of a little pregnant statuette, a phallus and testicles carved from chalk, and a mound of flint blocks and antler

25. Engraving of a red deer on a flint crust; Grimes Graves, Norfolk.

picks. Doubtless this offering was to placate the earth and make the next mine more fruitful; but the little fat goddess belongs to a family going back far beyond the Neolithic, into Palaeolithic times (see plate 26).

26. The chalk 'goddess' from Grimes Graves, Norfolk.

As well as these shadowy signs of the survival of an older way of life, however, there was a farming tradition in the British Isles which differed from the Windmill Hill culture, notably in making decorated pottery, and using chisel-shaped arrow-heads instead of the leaf-shaped Windmill Hill ones. Perhaps this different tradition was brought to Britain by farmers coming by a different route, across the north European plain, perhaps it developed in the British Isles, as a result of contact between the new settlers and the earlier hunters. What is clear is that once again the British Isles received people and ways of life from a wide area, up the western seaways, and across the Channel and North Sea, and that once again this made a melting pot of traditions, and produced a distinctive local blend.

The most striking and mysterious element in this mixed tradition is the building of 'Megalithic' monuments. (Megalithic, from the Greek means simply 'of large stones'). Megalithic buildings are of many kinds – from burial chambers under earthen mounds, to single standing stones, or avenues and rings of stones. They are widely distributed all over western Europe, especially along the Atlantic coasts from Scotland to Spain. They continued to be used, and built long after the end of the 'Neolithic' period; but it is soon after the original settlement of Neolithic farmers that they began, and the oldest Megalithic structures are, for the most part, tombs for collective burials, like the long barrows mentioned above. Megalithic tombs vary in their exact form; the most important division being between 'passage graves' in which a long narrow passage leads to a burial chamber in the heart of the mound, and 'gallery graves' in which the passage is wider, divided by stone partitions into stall-like compartments for the burials. Both types differ from the long barrows with wooden mortuary chambers which they supersede, in that they could be entered again once they were complete so that several generations of dead could have been laid in the same tomb. The technique used by the builders varied from place to place depending perhaps largely on the most available sort of stone. Thus some tombs use massive blocks of stone standing upright as walls, with other huge blocks laid across horizontally to make a roof. Some of the weirdest sights in Britain are these stone structures left standing bare, with the earthen mound that once covered them eroded away (see plate 27).

But more impressive still are tombs with their barrows still intact, like the West Kennet Long Barrow, or Wayland's Smithy, or Bryn Celli Dhu in Anglesey (see plate 28).

In parts of the country where smaller stones, or easily split

27. Trevethy Quoit.

28. The Entrance to Bryn Celli Dhu Passage grave, Anglesey.

stone was available, the tomb builders used dry stone walling as well as larger stones, and in the Orkneys and in Ireland there are tombs with corbelled roofs – that is roofs made by laying each layer of stones slightly jutting out over the layer beneath, and weighed down by earth on its outer end, the jutting overlap being extended till the remaining space is small enough to be covered with a single large stone. This technique produces a beehive shaped, domed interior, as in the superb tomb at Maeshowe on Orkney (see plate 29). Many megalithic tombs have a kind of forecourt, perhaps a ceremonial area, in front of the entrance; at Belas Kanp in Gloucestershire the forecourt is at one end of the barrow, with a false doorway in it; the burial chambers were entered from the side of the barrow.

Everywhere, whatever the variations in form, megalithic tombs have this much in common: they are collective burials, and they do not contain rich grave goods of any kind, such as would suggest buried chieftains – merely a few pots, a stone axe, a flint blade or two.

Associated with the megalithic tombs was a particular style of art. This consists of stylized eyes and eyebrows, and patterns of triangles, lozenges, chevrons and spirals, sometimes in forms in which experts see a very formalized representation of a goddess. These patterns are found carved on the stones of megalithic monuments, notably the superb corbelled grave at New Grange, in Ireland (see colour plates 5 and 6), and also on portable objects, like the decorated bone plaque from Jarlshof, Shetland (see plate 30). There are also a number of curious carved stone balls, found mainly in Scotland, which carry patterns like the 'eye motif' of megalithic art (see colour plate 7). Strangest of all are 'The Folkton Drums' – three chalk cylinders found in a child's grave at Folkton, in Yorkshire (see plate 31). The burial was of Bronze Age date, but the little drums are obviously of megalithic style, decorated with spirals, triangles, and the eye and eyebrow motif. Were these toys, one wonders, or talismans?

The megalithic tombs present us with a problem. Can they really have been built by simple early farmers with no knowledge of civilization and only the simplest tools? This problem becomes

29. The corbelling of the roof in the chamber at Maeshowe, Orkney.

more acute as our knowledge and understanding of these monuments increases. Thus it has recently come to light that the

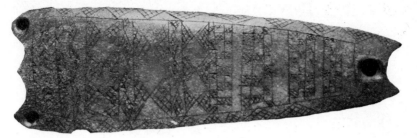

30. 'The Jarlshoff Plaque.'

passage grave at New Grange is aligned on the midwinter sunrise, in such a way that the rising sun throws a beam of light through a slit in the roof of the passage entrance and illuminates a spiral pattern carved on the chamber wall. New Grange is some thousand years older than Stonehenge, which is also aligned using astronomical knowledge. What inspired people to make such vast efforts – to devote their food surplus to the piling of huge quantities of earth, the heaving of massive stones? It used to be thought that the idea of building in stone, and of making impressive monuments for the dead had come ultimately from the Middle East, where, as we saw, farming had been invented, and where first villages, then towns, then urban civilization also emerged. Perhaps the barbarians of western Europe had been organized and instructed by visitors from eastern civilization – merchants looking for minerals, or, more likely, by missionaries, spreading the idea of such burials as part of a religion rather as Christian missionaries would thousands of years later produce a scatter of small churches. But the old picture has been severely shaken by a revolution in methods of dating – by 'the tree-ring calibration' of radiocarbon dates which you will find explained in Appendix I (page 114). The new dating pushes back the date of western European events compared with events in the Middle East and Aegean basin; it makes the megalithic tombs in Britain lie between 3,000 and 3,500 BC. They are therefore the oldest man-made stone structures known to us – older than the Pyramids. It is no use, then, explaining them in terms of superior visitors from outside.

31. 'The Folkton Drums.'

They must have been a distinctively western European development. The new dating is so recent a discovery that scholars have not yet had time to construct a new picture of the past in the light of it; but Professor Renfrew* has cautiously suggested that perhaps the megalithic tombs were built to mark the territory of particular clans of farmers – each group building the finest monument they could manage, as a form of family or local pride. The seaboard distribution of the tomb-building tradition would then arise, not because the idea was spread by seafarers along the coasts but because the slow migrations of farmers moving westwards in search of new land were halted by the Atlantic, so that pressure of population built up on the coastal lands, making such 'landmarks' desirable.

Megalithic tombs were not the only impressive structures made by Neolithic people in Britain. They also made 'cursus' and 'henge' monuments. A 'cursus' is two parallel ditches, which

---

* Renfrew: *Before Civilization.*

run for great distances, sometimes as much as several miles, across the landscape. They seem to be connected with long barrows – a famous one near Stonehenge is very obviously lined up with a long barrow at one end. Perhaps they had something to do with funeral ceremonies; nobody knows what they were for. Henges were almost certainly temples. In their earliest form they consisted of a circular bank and ditch, within which was a circle of pits, or an arrangement of timber posts, or stones. Of course the most famous henge is Stonehenge, and Stonehenge was first laid out by Neolithic farmers, but in its original form it was simply a circular bank and ditch, and a ring of pits, many of which contained cremated human bones.

The people who made these first lasting scars on our landscape remain themselves very shadowy. We know very little, for example, about their houses. They did not actually live in the causewayed camps they built, and at first did not live in villages either, perhaps because their lives, although more settled than the hunters, were not yet permanently rooted – their farming exhausted the soil very quickly, and they moved on to fresh fields. A few rectangular huts, apparently made of wattle and daub, with stone footings to the walls have been found, but nothing like the established villages of the Middle East and the Danube basin. But in the far north, on Orkney, a whole village has been found, preserved, covered in sand, on the shore (see plates 32, 33). Skara Brae is a group of stone-built huts, clustered together, and linked by passages which were roofed over with stone lintels, and led out to paved areas open to the sky. After it had been built the whole village was covered with debris, rubbish and soil, so that it must have looked from the outside like a bumpy little hill. This was probably done to keep out the ferocious winds that sweep Orkney, and which keep it bare of trees. Lacking wood the Skara Brae villagers made do with stone and whale-bone. Their houses are astonishingly well fitted out, with built-in beds each with its own little cupboards in the thickness of the wall, recessed hearths and boxes in the floor, and handsome dressers two storeys high. Small cells opened from the houses, some of them with covered drains in the floor; others, found full of fine

32. Skara Brae: General view.

33. Skara Brae, Orkney: Interior of hut.

beads and elaborately worked implements, were presumably storehouses. The Skara Brae villagers were using only stone tools. They raised cattle and sheep which must have flourished on the open pasture of their windswept island. There is no sign that they grew crops, or that fishing was important, except for the gathering of shellfish. They decked themselves with beads of teeth and bone, and small stone cups containing red, yellow, or blue pigment suggest that they painted their bodies.

Skara Brae raises the possibility that the more southerly Neolithic farmers whose land and resources were surely richer, may have lived in at least as adequate a style, though their furniture, like the houses would have been made of wood and has perished. And there is certainly much more to be learned. For example, a very recent excavation at Carn Brea near Redruth in Cornwall has discovered a true Neolithic village, surrounded by a massive granite wall, and containing terraces, each of roughly equal area, and apparently each containing one house. Outside the wall there are signs of fields. One wonders if the wall was defensive, and if so, against whom. Carn Brea is the oldest known village in England.

Afterthought

It would hardly be possible to exaggerate the changes that in the long run resulted from mankind's discovery of agriculture and animal husbandry. The greater certainty, and the greater abundance of food yielded by farming compared to hunting had the most far-reaching results. For example the amount of food obtainable by farming bore a more direct relationship to the amount of effort put into getting it, so that more people could get more food, whereas the amount of food available from hunting always depended on the habits of the hunted animals, and to hunt in a larger band might easily be a disadvantage. By enabling much larger groups of people to live together, farming paved the way towards increased specialization, for in the larger group there was not only a better chance of a food surplus to support craftsmen –

toolmakers, potters, or miners – but also a larger range of different human talents. The possibilities which this change opened up were very slow to be developed; doubtless for a very long time each family did everything for itself, and relied only seldom upon the special skills of others. Indeed, a high degree of self-sufficiency still marks the simplest farming people of the present day. And yet, even if they were miners only part of the time, the folk who dug flints at Grimes Graves, were obviously the owners of special skills, and the long path towards the nuclear physicist of the present day had been begun upon.

As well as being better provided with food, the farmer was more settled than the hunter. He had to stay in one spot at least until the harvest; and after the harvest he had to store his grain somewhere, and until the fertility of the soil was exhausted he needed to stay near his painfully cleared field. So the wandering life of the hunter whose house is temporary, whose property is all portable as he follows his game, was replaced by a more settled life. For the first time men lived in one patch of landscape, and made of one special place a permanent home. This change too was gradual, for primitive farmers quickly exhausted the soil and moved on; little by little they must have learned to rotate cultivation across a limited area, returning to land left fallow for a few years, and perhaps this knowledge arose first in western Europe, where the Atlantic halted the slow migration in search of fresh land. Surely the people who left the first enduring monuments on the face of the land, who built vast barrows and henges, felt local ownership and pride in the land they left their mark upon, and shared that love of one place more than any other which is still a common human emotion among us now.

This more settled and localized life was closely adapted to the different character and climate of different places, so that it is natural that the western European Neolithic should have a cultural pattern of its own, including the spectacular megalithic tombs.

The inventions of the Neolithic 'revolution' were not made all at once, yet each of them hastened the arrival of the others. A haunch of meat, for instance, can simply be roasted, but to cook porridge you need a cooking pot. Once you are exploiting plants, growing flax for its seeds, and acquiring fewer skins than a purely hunting people, the discovery that fibres from plants can be spun and woven will be more than welcome. In just such a way the existence of kilns for firing pottery facilitated the smelting of metals that marked the next great technical advance of mankind.

Before we leave the peaceful Neolithic farmers it is worth remarking that their basic way of life is still with us to a much greater extent than that of the hunters. Very large areas of the earth are tilled by peasant farmers, by methods which have not greatly changed since prehistoric times, except by the use of a little iron. Great cultures have depended on such farming for the food surplus on which their achievements rest. India, China, South America, and most of Africa are still largely farmed by simple peasants using only the most primitive tools, and the African Kraal in plate 34, must look very like a settlement of the earliest farmers. Far from being isolated survivals like the

34. An African Kraal, in Rhodesia.

remaining hunter food-gatherers of the earth, peasant farmers still provide much of the world with its food.

In exchange for greater security (though not perfect security, for harvests may fail) and greater stability (though not perfect stability, for the soil may fail), mankind accepted a life of ceaseless hard toil, devoid of the excitements and danger of the hunt, devoid of movement and adventure. Such a choice must have involved a price to pay in human welfare, as well as a gain. 'If the Great Spirit had intended men to be always in one place, he would have made the world stand still,' said Chief Flying Hawk. In the book of Genesis it is after man has been cast out of the Garden of Eden that he becomes a farmer. God says to Adam:

> 'Cursed is the earth in thy work; with labour and toil shalt thou eat thereof all the days of thy life. Thorn and thistles shall it bring forth to thee, and thou shalt eat the herbs of the earth. In the sweat of thy brow shalt thou eat bread . . .'

A life of hard work on the land, at the mercy of weather produces a quiet and stoical view of life in modern people who lead it, and probably did from the first. But though this life seems less attractive to modern eyes than that of the hunter we should not underestimate the achievements of the first farmers. They had religious beliefs surely at least as deep as those of their ancestors; we have seen that the old fertility cult of the hunters was continued into Neolithic times doubtless with renewed force now that it was the fertility of the earth itself that was involved. The Neolithic man also had the ability to organize with his fellows to accomplish great works in common, one of the rewards perhaps, of living in closer contact with more of his fellow human beings.

The distinctively human urge to change things which do not suit us can be traced back to the first ape who broke a smooth stone to get a cutting edge, but it has reached a new scale, a new self-confidence when it is the face of the land itself that is moulded to human use – when forests are cleared and great landmarks made. Perhaps, too, the first aesthetic artistic urges of mankind are to be seen in the handaxe whose beauty and symmetry of form are greater than they need to be for use; but in the magnificent interiors of megalithic tombs, and the strange unearthly symbolic art of spirals and eyes, the aesthetic urge reached a haunting significance worthy to be compared with the earlier achievements of the cave-painters, and indeed, in its hunger for mystery and grandeur, with the achievements of later, fully civilized periods.

FOUNDERS OF BRONZE

WE have now reached the dawn of another of the traditional epochs into which scholars divide prehistory – 'the Bronze Age'. The way forward for human societies lay in twin developments that each supported and encouraged the other – the development of metallurgy, and the development of cities, and therefore of true civilization. It used to be thought that the working of metals was discovered first by the advanced and already town-dwelling peoples of the Middle East, and spread from there into the Aegean basin to mainland Greece, and from there across Europe. It was thought that prospectors, searching for metal-bearing ores had carried with them the knowledge necessary for the extraction and working of metal, and passed it on to the people from whom the metal ore could be purchased by trade.

Two advances in modern knowledge of the past have left this traditional picture in ruins. First, the discovery of bronze turns out, like the 'Neolithic revolution', to have been a prolonged process rather than an abrupt change. A long 'Copper Age' preceded the discovery that a much tougher and more easily cast metal could be obtained by alloying copper with 10 per cent tin – which gives true bronze. And at first copper was used to make small things, awls, fish-hooks, pins and the like, which suggest that it was valued for its decorative qualities rather than for its improved strength.

Secondly the new dating techniques (see Appendix I) which as we have seen, disproved the theory that megalithic tombs in western Europe derived from the influence of eastern civilization, also threw the traditional theory of the Bronze Age into confusion. For example, metallurgy seems to have developed earlier in the Balkans than in the Aegean basin. For the history of the British Isles the main consequence of the new chronology is that we can no longer think of the bronze-using peoples of Wessex, the builders of the surviving form of Stonehenge among other achievements as having derived their knowledge and skill from contact with the famous civilization of Mycenae, for Stonehenge is older than the rise of Mycenae. It will be some time before the new dating and the old knowledge of prehistory are welded together to make a new coherent account of what happened; and no part of this book is more likely to need rewriting in a year or two than the following pages.

Copper occurs as native metal – small metallic lumps which are easily hammered into shapes like beads or rough tools – and it may well have attracted attention first for its decorative quality. The next step is the discovery that the metal can be melted and cast in moulds, then that it can be extracted from the ores in which it usually occurs by heating the ore in the right way. We can only speculate how these discoveries came to be made, though we may reasonably guess that the existence of kilns for firing pottery helped the discovery of smelting on its way. Pure copper is not easy to cast; the presence of other elements such as arsenic, which can occur naturally in copper ores, gives a better result. The early metallurgists eventually discovered that the addition of tin (the ideal proportion is 10 per cent) gave them a fine tough metal, easily cast, and capable of keeping a sharp cutting edge.

During the period after the invention of copper metallurgy, while the first urban life of Europe was slowly developing in the Aegean and in Greece, the rest of Europe was in a state of upheaval with great migrations of people taking place. Among the people on the move were the 'Beaker people' so called after the shape of their most characteristic pottery vessel. The migrations of these people were to bring them as invaders into southern Britain, the first metal-users to reach us. The Beaker people seem to have originated in Spain. Whether copper working had been

independently discovered there, or whether it reached them from
the far end of the Mediterranean, the Beaker people knew of it,
and worked it with some skill, as well as working gold. They
grew more barley than wheat – perhaps they had discovered how
to brew beer from barley, and that explains the shape and size of
their pottery. They made arrow-heads, knives and daggers in
fine flint work, and wrist guards (to protect the archer's wrist
from the recoil of the bowstring), from various sorts of stone.
They made buttons and beads from bone and jet, and ear-rings
like little baskets from gold (see plate 35).

35. Beaker grave goods from Radley, Berkshire, and from Dorchester and
Stanton Harcourt, Oxon.

From Spain these talented people seem to have moved northwards and eastwards in mainland Europe, and then in a later
movement to have returned westwards, and settled the accessible
regions of southern Britain. On their wanderings they had come
into contact with another wandering group, which had spread all
over eastern and northern Europe, and had its origin perhaps in

the Kurgan culture of the south Russian steppes. This second group of people, called the Battle-axe people, made pottery decorated by impressing cords into the wet clay; they used wheeled carts, had domesticated the horse, and were workers in copper. They are named from the finely ground and polished perforated stone axes which accompany their burials, and suggest that they were warriors as much as farmers (see plate 36). They buried their dead in single graves, often under round barrows, much smaller than the great long barrows of Neolithic times. The Battle-axe people are of great interest because they may have been the bearers of a 'proto Indo-European' language (see Appendix II, page 119).

Shortly after 3,000 BC the Beaker people and the Battle-axe people met and mingled in the Low Countries, and the Beakers found in the British Isles belong to this mixed tradition. The wandering newcomers evidently mixed readily enough with any strangers they encountered, for their already mongrel culture mixed also with that of the Neolithic farmers they found in

36. Shaft-hole axes of the battle-axe culture from Denmark.

Britain – bell-beakers are often found in megalithic tombs, and in association with the 'henge' temples of Neolithic farmers. A little later there emerged in Britain a new form of pottery – the 'food vessel' shape, which looks as if it arises from a blend of Beaker traditions with the decorated pottery made by the non-Windmill Hill farmers.

The Beaker people adopted and improved the existing temple at Stonehenge – remarkable proof that they had mixed with the earlier inhabitants, and shared ideas with them – by erecting within its circumference two concentric settings of huge stones. For some reason beyond our ken these stones, the famous 'blue-stones' were not found near by, though there was no shortage of large stones locally, but were brought from the Prescelly mountains in Wales, an operation which must have involved an enormous output of organized effort and man-hours. The entrance to this new circle was aligned on the midsummer sunrise.

At Avebury the Beaker people made another great henge monument, much more impressive than Stonehenge, though less well preserved. Avebury is a vast circular ditch and bank, within which was a ring of standing stones – originally there were about a hundred of them. Within this outer ring were two smaller circles of stones, and outside the monument was a long avenue of stones leading for more than a mile southwards. A village now lies partly within the temple, and many of the stones are gone (see plate 37).

Close by Avebury rises Silbury Hill (see plate 38) like a huge green pudding, the largest man-made mound in prehistoric Europe. It has been calculated that Silbury Hill took 18 million man-hours to construct; it can be dated around 2,500 BC. This awesome and mysterious monument was probably built at the same time as the temple at Avebury; if it is not a burial mound no one knows what it is; yet no burial has yet been found in it.

Clearly the copper-using people who produced the spectacular achievements of construction described above, and many others, were in some ways unlike the Neolithic peoples with whom they had mixed. They were, for one thing, more warlike, as their battle-axes show, and more interested in individuals, as their

37. Avebury from the air.

habit of burying single people, and of putting grave goods in the burial mounds shows us. Yet they were at least as ready as earlier people to combine together on huge public works, to dig, heave,

38. Silbury Hill, Wiltshire.

transport and erect vast sarsens, or, at Silbury, actually to make a
hill by the labour of their hands. What were the Beaker people
like? We do not know very much about them apart from what
they built. They must have commanded very large surpluses of
food, at least during some times of the year, to be able to devote
so many man-hours on construction. The scarcity of dwelling
sites suggests that on their wanderings across Europe they had
come to depend more on animal husbandry than on arable farming – herds are after all more movable than standing crops.
And the alignment of Stonehenge on the midsummer sunrise
has been held to show that it was among them that some sort of
sun-religion began to supplant the old fertility cult of the mother-
goddess; certainly the burials suggest a male-dominated as well
as a warlike society; however, as we saw, the alignment on a
sunrise was not new, but had been done at New Grange long
before.

From among these talented people of mixed cultural tradition
there was to arise a still more spectacular culture – the so-called
'Wessex Culture'. The 'Wessex Culture' is the name given to a
number of burials with very rich grave goods, under round barrows in southern Britain. The grave goods include well-made
stone battle-axes, metal daggers with hilts decorated richly, sometimes in gold, and precious ornaments of gold or amber (see plate
39). Some of the loveliest prehistoric objects to be found in
Britain come from Wessex culture graves, like the amber cup
from Hove (see colour plate 9) or the splendid gold cup from
Rillaton (see colour plate 10) which is so like golden cups found
at Mycenae that it used to be quoted to prove the existence of
trade between Greece and Wessex. In a number of graves there
were amber discs edged with gold, that might have been sun-
amulets, and in a famous burial under 'Bush Barrow' near Stonehenge there was also a 'sceptre', a rod decorated with bone
mounts, and with a polished mace-head at one end (see colour
plate 8). The individuals who were buried with such splendour
were obviously rich and important also in life; the first wealthy
people in Britain.

It is to the rich and magnificent culture of the Wessex burial

39. Grave goods from a 'Wessex Culture' burial on Manton Down, Wiltshire. Notice the gold-bound amber disc (a sun-amulet?) and the miniature halberd pendant.

that the erection of the final form of Stonehenge is attributed – that form of which the ruins are still visible today. This unique and amazing structure was built after the complete removal of the bluestone ring, of which some of the stones were later re-used. The new ring is made of huge sarsen stones, which came, most probably from the region of Avebury, some 30 miles away. These stones were not just used in a raw state, but shaped and dressed; then curved lintel stones (see plate 40) were by some means, perhaps with ramp and roller, perhaps using a wooden cradle gradually built up beneath them, raised and placed across the

40. Stonehenge; the curvature of the lintel stones.

uprights to form the circle still partly standing now. The stones were held in position ingeniously; on the top of the uprights a projecting boss was left (see plate 41) which fitted into sockets on the under side of the lintel stones. This newer structure, which must have been immensely grand when complete (see plate 42), preserved the alignment of the bluestone circle on the midsummer sunrise, and indeed there are other possible astronomical alignments of the stones, to predict the movement of moonrise, and the occurrence of eclipses which have been suggested by modern scholars.

We might consider for a moment the sort of society that was capable of building Stonehenge. Not only must the people in such a society have been efficient farmers, capable of producing a large food surplus to feed the work-teams that hauled and dressed and heaved the massive stones, they must also have had some experts, a group of learned men who had the knowledge necessary

41. Stonehenge; the tenon on stone 56.

to build what is, in effect, an astronomical observatory. Probably there were priests, or wise men who accumulated this knowledge over generations; they too would need to live on a food surplus from the labour of others. Of course it is not necessary to suppose that they could work out *in advance* exactly where sunrise or moonrise would occur on particular days; they may have set up the stones to mark the places where it happened, as it happened, so that Stonehenge is a record of observations made – a kind of architectural writing, rather than a prediction of what might happen in years to come. But even so the amount of knowledge needed to know which astronomical events are significant, and to predict them accurately enough to be ready to mark them out on the ground was a considerable achievement, especially since there was no writing to help remember and transmit this knowledge. Clearly the society that could afford to accumulate the knowledge behind Stonehenge, and expend the effort that went into building it, was a wealthy society: and if Stonehenge was indeed the creation of the Wessex culture we know that its builders also had personal wealth – weapons, ornaments and drinking cups of great splendour (see colour plate 10).

Now there is an understandable reason for the wealth of

42. Artist's reconstruction of Stonehenge after its final rebuilding,
circa 2,000 BC.

southern Britain in the early Bronze Age, and that is the position
of the chalk uplands on possible trade routes. True bronze
requires tin which is a rare metal but abundantly present in
Cornwall, and once metal-working became widespread there was
also a demand for gold, which is found in the mountains of Wales,
and was plentifully available in Ireland. Until recently, noticing
certain similarities between objects found in Wessex graves, and
objects found in Mycenaean contexts in Greece, scholars were
inclined to think that there had been a well-established trade link
between Britain and the flourishing urban and literate Mycenaeans, and that it was from Greece that the inspiration and knowledge for Stonehenge had come. Perhaps the Rillaton cup (see
colour plate 10) was a present from a Greek chieftain to a Cornish
one . . . perhaps the dagger-shaped carvings on some of the
Stonehenge uprights were the signature of a Mycenaean archi-
tect . . . but the new dating discussed in Appendix I makes this
more or less impossible, for Stonehenge in its third and most

elaborate form was complete before the rise of Mycenae. We must now suppose that the knowledge and ambition behind Stonehenge, and Avebury, and Silbury, were of native growth. Of course it is still likely that the wealth and power of the Wessex chieftains came from trade in gold and tin, and that the trade routes they so dominated reached far across Europe. Their prosperity was not short-lived; rich burials continue in southern Britain until about 1,500 B C.

The middle and late Bronze Age of Britain is harder to describe. There was a change in burial customs, from inhumation to cremation, with the ashes buried in an inverted pottery urn, under a barrow. Field agriculture grew in importance, and it is from the middle Bronze Age that the first known traces of field systems and plough marks survive. A light plough of some kind was in use, and farming seems to have been on a larger scale than before. There was a good deal of development in bronze technology; new shapes were produced for axes, to make them easier to fit to handles. In Wessex times flanges had been made along the sides of axes, and now there were longer and narrower axeheads, called 'Palstaves' often with a loop for a binding of some kind, and with larger flanges. Sometimes the flanges were enlarged till they could be hammered round to enclose the haft (see plate 43). Finally in the middle Bronze Age the socketed axe

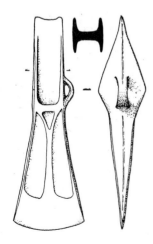

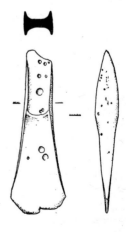

43. Various axe-shapes
in use, middle to late
Bronze Age.
(continued on page 76)

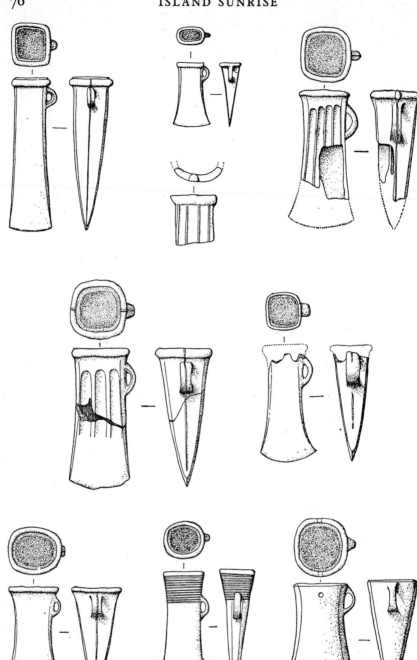

came into use; this was an axe made hollow at one end so that the handle could be inserted in it; making such axes involved casting in a two-part mould with a core, a notable advance in the bronze-founder's skill. At this time also pointed swords for thrusting replaced the Wessex daggers, and the first slashing swords – with cutting edges on both sides – appear (see plate 44), and also well-made spearheads, often provided with loops like the axe-heads.

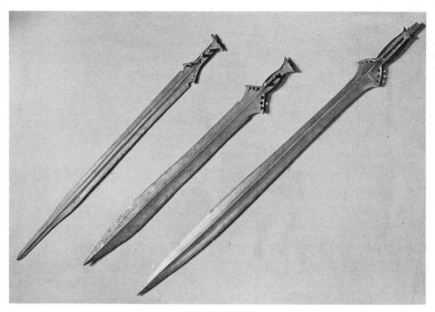

44. Swords of the later Bronze Age from the Thames.

Gold working also flourished, and there are beautiful torques and armlets from the middle Bronze Age (see plates 45, 46), and even a huge sheet-gold cape, finely decorated, surely the mark of a chieftain (see plate 47). Not only gold was used for ornament; elaborate necklaces also survive, of amber in the south, and in northern Britain more usually in jet (see plate 48).

This broad picture of increasing mastery in the making of an increasing variety of objects continues into the later Bronze Age.

In the eastern Mediterranean both the Hittite kingdom and the Mycenaean fell, around 1,200–1,150 BC. At the same time there appeared in central Europe a group of cultures who buried their dead not under barrows, but in flat cemeteries, cremated in urns.

45. Massive gold collar from Moulsford, Berkshire, made of four twisted rods, and weighing about 1 lb.

These 'Urnfield' cultures had very sophisticated bronze working, and obtained their copper ore by large-scale mining. The size of their cemeteries suggests they were supporting a dense and expanding population. Bronze was more plentiful, perhaps because after the cataclysm that had overtaken the Mycenaeans less of it was being traded south, and it was now used to make commonplace tools in great variety – chisels, saws, sickles and such like, and perhaps ploughshares. Spreading from their original homelands in Hungary and Czechoslovakia, and Austria, the Urnfield peoples triggered other movements of peoples, and so by migration and by trade their ideas and techniques spread widely over Europe. Whether or not Urnfield peoples actually migrated and settled in the British Isles, some of their innovations in metal working reached here, notably the new technique

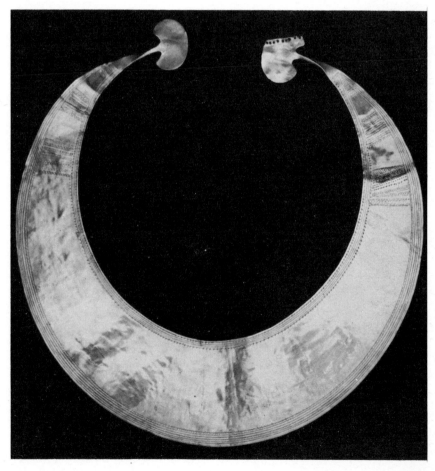

46. Gold collar, of the form called 'lunula' from Auchtentaggart, Dumfries

for obtaining sheets of bronze by repeatedly heating and hammering. Sheet bronze was then used to make cauldrons and bowls, shields and helmets (see plates 49, 50) and even musical instruments, like the bronze horns of which several have been found in Ireland.

47. Sheet gold cape from Mold, Flintshire.

Numerous hordes of bronze implements have been discovered in Britain, some of them, like the one from Wilburton, Cambridgeshire, consisting of worn and broken items, presumably collected by a bronze smith for melting down and recasting. There are other indications of a general improvement in practical crafts – loom weights are found and even fragments of textile, so that the era of dependence on skins was passing. At North Ferriby, Yorkshire, a complex, plank-built boat was found. It was about 50 feet long, and 8 feet wide. The timbers were carefully jointed, lashed together with yew withies, and caulked. Very fine gold ornaments were still being made.

The late Bronze Age was a time of settled farming communities

8. Objects from the Bush Barrow, near Stonehenge

9. A drinking cup carved in solid amber,
nearly 4 inches across

10. Gold cup from Rillaton, Cornwall

using plough agriculture, and animal husbandry, and almost certainly with specialist metal workers in each community replacing the wandering tinkers of earlier times. Finally, and significant of the kind of changes that had been taking place in society, it is from the end of the Bronze Age that some of the hill-forts which are so conspicuous a feature of the English landscape began to be built.

48. Multistrand necklace of jet, with spacer beads, from Aberlemno, Angus.

But long before the Bronze Age drew to a close in Britain, the Iron Age had begun elsewhere.

49. Cauldron in sheet bronze from West of Scotland, capable of
holding over 10 gallons.

Afterthought

Confronted with the new dating we must try to see the achievements of the Bronze Age in a new light. When some time has
passed archaeologists will draw up a new picture in the light of
all the evidence, old and new; in the meantime it is at least clear
that we should regard the Bronze Age in our islands as a local
growth, instead of explaining everything by reference to traders
from Mycenae. That we should find this so difficult is itself an
interesting cultural fact; we are very impressed by the cultural
achievements of cities. Our very word for advanced culture –
'civilization' is a give-away, for it means 'belonging to cities'.

The development of cities which began in the Near East, and in the Bronze Age spread to the Aegean basin, was a distinctively eastern and Mediterranean solution to the problem of how to organize society. This line of development ultimately gave us the cities of classical Greece, and the enormous power of Rome; like the Greeks and the Romans we are inclined to think of other life-styles as 'barbarian', and to suppose that barbarian peoples can achieve very little.

Yet in the 'barbarian' and remote British Isles, there existed already in Neolithic times some system for organizing work on great public monuments. Neolithic societies were capable of building barrows, causewayed camps, henges, which must have involved hundreds of man-hours. The increasingly ambitious achievements of the Bronze Age are only a continuation of that. What we are probably seeing in the archaeological record is a 'barbarian' society of increasingly organized chiefdoms. It is possible to regret the emergence of chiefs, and to think that the

50. Two fine bronze shields from Auchmaleddie and Yetholm in Scotland could only have been intended for use as parade items as they were hammered up from a single sheet of bronze with only edge strengthening and a separate central umbo.

personal wealth, and therefore the inequality of the society of the Wessex graves was a backward step. We are used to thinking of equality as a good thing, so that less of it must be bad. But increasingly things were within the scope of human achievement which could not be within the scope of each individual person. The most striking example of this is the astronomical knowledge that went into building Stonehenge; metallurgy is a more basic example. The skills needed for smelting ores, alloying, casting and annealing, cannot be developed by a farmer in his spare time. To reach a level of skill in these exacting crafts a man had to specialize; if society was to enjoy the use of bronze artifacts it had to be organized to allow that. It is not only that the craftsman must eat food provided by the labour of others, but that there must be some way of distributing what he makes among others.

Just as the distribution across the British Isles of polished stone axes was probably effected not by 'trade' in the modern sense, but by the exchange of ceremonial gifts, so now the redistribution of food and goods was probably effected by making tribute to a chieftain. This man would receive a share of the produce of different kinds of all his tribe, and then would share it out – giving it out as gifts to his subjects. In return for his generosity they owed him services – fighting for him if need be, or working at his command on the huge monuments that so dramatically remain. It is even possible, from the distribution of long barrows, causewayed camps and henges to discern possible territories for Wessex chieftains, in each of which lay one major henge monument. Although the power and glory of the chieftain of Wessex clans must have been great, and celebrated doubtless in songs and stories long since lost to us, their *function* in society was as necessary and humble as that of the handful of coins and notes in your pocket, which enable you to exchange work at one occupation (for which you are paid) for goods made by someone else (which you buy).

How were these chieftainships organized? Since there was no city to act as a permanent nexus there must surely have been periodical gatherings of the people – a 'Folkmoot' – at certain times of the year. There is some evidence of wooden houses within the henges; were these the dwellings of the chief, or of his priests (or was priest and chief the same man?) Perhaps the henges were the places at which the people gathered together. A need to fix the time of such gatherings – as of other essential operations like seed-time and harvest, could explain the need for the astronomical sightings from Stonehenge.

In one way we could say that a society capable of building the henge monuments was a wealthy one; we have seen that in the early Bronze Age there was a sudden increase in another kind of wealth – the ownership by one person of splendid articles of property – cups and daggers, buttons, and amulets, torques of gold and suchlike. It is surely no coincidence that the dagger is found so widely in these wealthy burials. Once individuals were wealthy they were worth looting; the increasing wealth generated by metal-working, and the increasing application of bronze technology to making weapons go together. Self-respect and self-defence both required each man to be as well armed as his neighbours; in the Aegean there seems to have been a kind of arms race to possess metal daggers which must have greatly stimulated the earliest demand for bronze.

In imagining this society of farmers, villagers, and petty princes, with their courts, and their warlike bands we have a picture of human society which suddenly comes into focus. Many of the features of it are paralleled closely in historical times. The duty to give working hours to a prince, for example, is like the duty to help with earthworks owed to an Anglo-Saxon king by his subjects; periodic assembly is like the folkmoot or the Icelandic All-thing. The distributive function of the chief's court might bring to mind the extravagant praise in Beowulf for a generous lord – a 'ring-giver', and so on.

Such chieftains provided the patronage necessary for the maker of gold ornaments, for the bronze worker, and doubtless for other fine craftsmen, among them almost certainly, the poet. For in Bronze Age Europe we find ourselves in the world of Homer; the world of *Beowulf*, and the Sagas, and the Welsh and Irish heroic poetry. The roots of our oldest surviving literature reach back to, and illuminate, this level of the past. Compared to the stable, and communal life of cities this world of petty powers making war was doubtless insecure, bloody and changeable; still it led eventually, as it grew more elaborate and more tightly regulated, to the feudal societies of medieval Europe. And our own society is derived from it, as well as from Greece and Rome.

MEN OF IRON

A KNOWLEDGE of iron did not follow naturally from a knowledge of bronze working, for the two techniques are very different. Iron must be smelted in a furnace; the pieces of metal must then be picked out and heated again to fuse them into a single large lump, and this can then be 'forged' – shaped by heating and hammering. In prehistoric times no means existed to heat iron sufficiently to make it possible to cast it in moulds, and the technical knowledge so laboriously built up for the production of elaborate objects in bronze could not be applied to it. But it had two immense advantages; it is stronger than bronze, and the ore from which it is obtained is very plentiful and occurs very widely, unlike the scarce tin needed for bronze. From the first, therefore, iron could be used for workaday objects, for saws, nails and ploughshares, as well as for weapons.

Iron working was at first a closely guarded military secret of the Hittite Empire, in Asia Minor. Knowledge of it began to spread when the Hittite Empire was overthrown, shortly after 1,200 BC. This was a period of migration and upheaval, which led to the collapse of Mycenae also, and ushered in the Dark Ages between Mycenae and classical civilization in Greece. By the eighth century BC both the city states of classical Greece, the Phoenicians, and the Etruscans were emerging in the Mediterranean area. In central Europe, the 'Urnfield' culture, which had prospered in the late Bronze Age, continued to develop and prosper, now benefiting from another local resource which began to be a valuable commodity, and which could be mined in

'Urnfield' lands – salt. In the Urnfield regions a new culture gradually developed in the seventh and sixth centuries BC – the iron-using culture known as 'Hallstatt' after a site in Austria.

The most significant element in the new culture was the practice of burying important men with rich grave goods, including a wheeled wagon, in a timber-built burial chamber under an earthen barrow. These burials are so different from the 'Urnfield' burials that it is natural to look for some influence from elsewhere to account for them, and the place that suggests itself is the Russian steppes, where burials containing carts or wheels date back as far as the third millennium BC. In that region too, horses had already been tamed for riding and pulling vehicles; in Urnfield and Hallstatt times there are plentiful finds of horse-harness of eastern type – bits, and attachments. Clearly the Hallstatt people were in contact with the south Russian region. There is a known historical event which may account for this – the expansion of the Scyths, who dislodged their neighbours, the Cimmerians, and began a migration westwards. Under pressure from the east the Hallstatt peoples spread across Austria, Switzerland, and south-west Germany, and then into France and Belgium, finally reaching, or at least influencing, the British Isles.

The Hallstatt people were bearers of a rich, varied and technically skilled culture; plentiful gold ornaments are found in their graves, and though their fine long swords were of iron, they still used bronze for many things. They made fine pottery, shaped to imitate metal forms, and burnished to a shiny surface. They used a geometric style of decoration, accompanied by little cast model animals of great charm (see plate 51).

The earliest British Iron Age sites are in the south and east, and are little changed from late Bronze Age settlements. They still use round houses, like Bronze Age farmers, and had not adopted the rectangular houses of the Hallstatt people. But objects were in use which are of Hallstatt type, like some bronze razors from Staple Howe, for example, and they were using iron for small objects, like pins. It is not known whether the iron users came in large numbers as invaders, or in small numbers as traders or conquering chieftains, or whether the knowledge of

51. A cow and her calf, cast in solid bronze from the rim of a bowl from Hallstatt, upper Austria.

iron was spread together with a trade in iron objects. But how far from the Hallstatt homelands the influence of their style could reach may be seen by looking at the charming though baffling object (see plate 52) of unknown use, found in Co. Antrim in Ireland.

Meanwhile, however, the Hallstatt peoples on the continent were trading with, and influenced by, the higher civilizations of the classical world – the ancient Etruscans, and, after the founding of the Greek colony of Massilia (Marseilles) at the mouth of

52. Goad? from Dunaverney, County Antrim.

the Rhone, with the Greeks themselves. Finds of buckets and strainers, and cups suggest that it was a northern taste for southern wine that sustained this flourishing trade. Under classical influence the Hallstatt culture blossomed, and developed into 'La Tene'.'La Tene', called after a site in Switzerland, is a name given, not to a fresh culture or way of life, but to an art style, flowering among the Hallstatt peoples – 'The first conscious art style to be created north of the Alps'.*

This art was a decorative art, in which embellishment of the surface of many kinds of object was achieved by the use of curvilinear patterns of great vigour, beauty and subtlety. The forms of animals, faces, and leaves were also used, but were treated as patterns. This style reached its pinnacle in the working of objects of gold and bronze and produced some of the most beautiful and desirable objects in the world (see plate 53). On the Continent the La Tene style came into existence around the mid-fifth century BC and lasted, with certain changes of style into the first century AD until the Roman occupation of its homelands. But in the British Isles it lasted until the first century AD, and continued in Ireland and perhaps in less romanized districts of Britain for many centuries after that. It outlasted the Roman occupation, to blend with Anglo-Saxon art, and deeply to influence the early Christian art of the Book of Kells in Ireland, or the English Lindisfarne Gospels.

We know from classical writers, and from later history that the people who created these superb objects were Celts, as probably were the Hallstatt people before them. And the time and manner of their arrival in this country are of great interest, for

* T. G. E. Powell: *Prehistoric Art.*

53. A superb pair of flagons, in bronze with coral inlay, in La Tene style, from Basse Yutz, Lorraine.

of all the invading peoples who have figured in this book they are the first whose culture and language survive here, however much changed, to the present day. The Irish, the Welsh, the Cornish and the Highland Scots present in a greater or lesser degree cultures which go back continuously to that of the ancient Celts. Much as we would like to know how and when they came the subject is difficult and obscure. There are two forms of Celtic spoken in our islands – Q-Celtic, in which the original Indo-European* Q sound is unchanged, and P-Celtic, in which it has altered to P. Irish is a Q-Celtic language, as are Scots Gaelic and Manx; Welsh, Cornish and Breton are P-Celtic. But we do not

* See Appendix II.

know what pattern of wanderings and settlements brought about this distribution of languages, nor even, with any certainty when they arrived in Britain. It has even been suggested that the first Celtic speakers in Britain were the Beaker peoples, among whom the Wessex culture arose. Certainly what we know about the Wessex culture fits well enough with the kind of society described in the oldest Irish literature, which has very ancient roots. But archaeology has nothing certain to tell us about languages, and it is more usual to suppose that Celtic reached Britain along with iron, around 600 BC. From then until the coming of the Romans there were successive waves of Celtic immigration into Britain.

It was not only towards Britain that the Celtic people migrated from central Europe. They raided as far as Rome in 390 BC; they sacked Delphi, in mainland Greece in 278 BC. An army of some 20,000 of them crossed into Asia Minor, and founded the colony of Galatia. At about 300 BC when their power was at its height, an enormous territory, from Galatia to Ireland was Celtic, and shared a largely common culture. And because of their contacts with the literate classical world, we know a good deal about them. It is worth noticing that this evidence – passages of description of Celtic ways of life, coming from literary sources, is the first 'historical' evidence we have been able to use in this book.

From Caesar, for example, in Book I of the *Gallic Wars* we learn that the mass of people among the Celts in Gaul were treated as little better than slaves, while there were two privileged classes – Druids, and Knights. The Druids acted as priests in religious ceremonies, and as judges in disputes large or small. They possessed a large body of traditional learning which had to be learned by heart by young men wishing to become Druids, so that sometimes the necessary study could take 20 years. There was a taboo upon writing down druidic lore, though for such humdrum purposes as keeping accounts, the Celts in Gaul knew and used the Greek alphabet. The Knights, the other class of privileged men, took the field with all their servants and retainers whenever there was a need for war. The possession of a following of men, large or small, was the only kind of position or power recognized amongst them.

This is what Strabo tells us of the Celts of Gaul:

'The whole race, which is now called Gallic, or Galatic, is madly fond of war, high-spirited and quick to battle, but otherwise straight-forward, and not of evil character. And so when they are stirred up they assemble in their bands for battle, quite openly, and without forethought, so that they are easily handled by those who desire to outwit them, for at any time or place, and on whatever pretext you stir them up you will have them ready to face danger, even if they have nothing on their side but their own strength and courage. On the other hand if won over by gentle persuasion they willingly devote their energies to useful pursuits, and even take to a literary educa-tion . . . To the frankness and high-spiritedness of their temperament may be added the traits of childish boastfulness and love of decora-tion. They wear ornaments of gold, torques on their necks, and bracelets on their arms and wrists, while people of high rank wear dyed garments, besprinkled with gold. It is this vanity which makes them unbearable in victory, and so completely cast down in defeat . . .'*

And here is an account from Diodorus of the Gauls in battle:†

'For their journeys and in battle they use two horse chariots, the chariot carrying both the charioteer and the chieftain (see plate 54). When they meet with cavalry in battle, they cast their javelins at the enemy, and then descending from the chariot, join battle with their swords. Some of them so far despise death that they descend to do battle unclothed except for a girdle. They bring into battle as their attendants free-men chosen from among the poorer classes, whom they use as charioteers and shield-bearers in battle. When the armies are drawn up in battle array they are wont to advance before the battle line, and to challenge the bravest of their opponents to single

* Strabo IV. iv. 2, 4. Translated by J. J. Tierney.
† The Celtic ethnography of Posidonious. Proceedings of the Royal Irish Academy, LX C5 1960.

combat, at the same time brandishing before them their arms, so as to terrify their foe. And when someone accepts their challenge to battle, they loudly recite the deeds of valour of their ancestors, and proclaim their own valorous quality, at the same time abusing and making little of their opponent, and generally attempting to rob him beforehand of his fighting spirit.'*

54. Celtic chariots: a reconstruction in use. Built by Felicity Kinross for B.B.C. Schools Television.

From other passages we learn of Celtic feasts – the diners seated on wolfskins on the floor, and served by 'their youngest grown-up children, both girls and boys'. The picture that emerges from classical writers, in short, is of a barbarian society, organized on a simple pattern in which tribes were governed by the assembled free citizens, with a council, and the chieftain was

* op. cit.

elected. The basic population were farmers or craftsmen; the aristocracy were warriors; priests and poets were held in high esteem. This is very much the sort of society which we guessed might account for the archaeological record of the Bronze Age; it is like the society reflected in Irish heroic literature, which preserves very ancient elements. But the picture derived from classical writers is more colourful than this, and tells us not only how the Celts on the continent were organized, but what they were like. They were brave and gay; high-spirited and unstable in temperament, loving poetry and learning, delighting in display.

The arrival of the Celts in Britain seems not to have been a sudden cataclysmic invasion, or large scale migration. It seems rather that they came in successive small waves, and, as so often before in this account, by different routes, carrying variant forms of the new culture, which once here blended with each other and the earlier native culture. Britain was placed so that it naturally received the tail-end of movements across the north European plain, or Celtic peoples coming north-westwards, displaced by the advance through Gaul of the expanding Roman Empire. The earliest 'Hallstat' influenced, iron-using tradition to arrive in Britain occupied the south and east; the later 'La Tene' bearing peoples seem to have found an easier foothold in the north-east, and south-west.

Two of many infiltrations of Britain can be most clearly distinguished after the first iron-users, and before the Belgae, who were the last pre-Roman invaders of these islands. First there are the La Tene chariot burials of Yorkshire, called 'The Arras Culture' from a cemetery at Arras near Beverley, Yorks. This culture is clearly an offshoot of the culture of the Marne valley in northern France, where a wealthy and flourishing La Tene people buried their dead in a similar manner with grave goods including chariots. There is also evidence of cross-Channel influence between Brittany and the south-west, doubtless sustained by the tin trade: a form of hill-fort began to be built in Cornwall which is also found in Brittany – a neck of land jutting into the sea was defended on the landward side by an earthwork wall (see plate 55).

55. The Rumps Cliff Castle, Cornwall.

Hill-forts of one kind or another sprung up all over Britain during the Iron Age. They are among the most spectacular relics of prehistory still visible in the landscape of Britain, crowning so many hills with mysterious grassy rings of ditch and mound. Hill-forts are also found on the continent, and their presence in such numbers in Britain doubtless reflects the disturbances caused by the movements of La Tene peoples into and around Britain. The hill-forts, however, differ so greatly in size and plan that they cannot all have served the same purpose. Some were occupied only in times of danger, when people and livestock took shelter inside them. Others housed a small group of people all the time – perhaps the local chieftain and his retainers; while some of the largest showed signs of having been lived in permanently for long periods, and even of containing workshops. These last must have been almost small townships, serving as markets and administrative centres for local tribes. When the sling was invented extra rings of ditches were added to many forts, to increase the distance between defenders and attackers, producing the spectacular 'Multivallate' forts, like Wareham Plateau Fort, or Maiden Castle (see plates 56, 57).

The people who took refuge in these great fortifications were at home in peaceful times in simple farming settlements. At Little

12. Superb shield found at Battersea. Originally the bronze was gilded, and red glass was set into the bronze mountings

13. Pair of bronze armlets with inset red and yellow enamelling from Castle Newe, Aberdeenshire

14. Magnificent early Iron age gold torque,
from Snettisham, Norfolk

15. Belgic coins of Cunobelin, the Catuvellaunian prince,
minted at Colchester (Camulodunum). Abbreviations of
these names, CVNO and CAMV, appearing on them

56. Wareham Plateau Fort, Norfolk.

Woodbury, for example, a large farmhouse has been excavated. It was round, and defended by a palisade. There were animal pens, and storage pits for grain. At Chysauster, in Cornwall, there is a village with stone-built huts, reminiscent of Skara Brae. Nine houses line a narrow street, with a few other houses scattered farther off. Each house had its own garden plot. The houses were built of low stone walls, and each had a courtyard open to the sky.

57. Maiden Castle, Dorset, from the air.

Opening off the courtyard was a living hut, with a hearth, and sometimes a granite basin for grinding corn. Around the courtyard were also long narrow work or store rooms, and stabling for beasts. There were covered drains beneath the floors. A track from the village led to a stream, where tin-washing was carried out (see plate 58).

58. Artist's impression of the Iron Age village at Chysauster, Cornwall.

Another well-known western settlement is the 'Lake Village' at Glastonbury, Somerset. This village consisted of wooden houses on the margin of a lake. A canoe was found, but as well as probably fishing, the inhabitants were farmers. In addition to fine metal work the Glastonbury villagers made very good pottery, decorated with curving lines in a La Tene style (see plate 59),

59. Fine pottery decorated in La Tene style,
from the Somerset lake villages.

and were accomplished carpenters, using a turning lathe, and mortice and tenon joints. Weaving equipment was recovered from their village too.

The economy of these Iron Age villages was based on mixed farming. Oats were grown, and a new sort of wheat, hardier in wetter conditions, although barley was still the chief crop in many places. In parts of England it is still possible from the air to distinguish the field systems of the iron age settlement (plate

60). Farmsteads were basically similar to those of the Bronze Age, but large circular huts surrounded by farm outbuildings take the place of several separate huts. These large thatched, and wattle and daub houses were sometimes surrounded by a palisade. They suggest prosperous families, farming large estates. Iron tools doubtless made agriculture easier, and there is some evidence now for rotation of crops, and dressing the soil with chalk, which would have helped to keep the land productive. Animal hus-

60. Celtic fields on Windover Hill, Sussex.

bandry had advanced too, and the large number of leaf-knives and billhooks suggests a wholesale gathering of vegetables for winter feeding of livestock. In highland and moorland areas stockbreeding was the main support of the tribes.

If the hill-forts were not witness enough, we should still surmise that the people of the Celtic Iron Age were always fighting from the vast numbers of weapons and war-gear recovered by archaeology. Numerous swords, daggers, spears, slingstones, war-chariots, shields and helmets have survived. Yet the artistic achievement of these warlike folk was in no way inferior to that of the continent. The La Tene art style flourished in Britain, at first in a style like that of continental art (see plate 61) and later developing a style of its own. Superb examples of

61. The Brentford Horncap. Probably an ornamented finial for a chariot yoke.

the metal-worker's art were created in Celtic Britain. Look at
plates 62 and 63, and colour plates 11, 12, 13 and 14. Notice the
mirrors particularly, for though they are based on Roman proto-

62. The 'Mayer' mirror.

types from Gaul, the shape, and the style of decoration are unique to Britain, and the simple and lovely flowing lines of the decoration on them show the La Tene style at its height. The taste these objects were wrought to please was not 'barbaric' in the modern sense of the word, but highly sophisticated. Abstract beauty of line, a liking for graceful circles and spirals, balanced but not mechanically symmetrical, pleasure in the interplay of light and shade on swelling plastic shapes, on the contrasting burnished and textured areas of the mirror-backs, or on the complex shapes of torques and armlets, demonstrate for us at once both the fine aesthetic taste of the owners of these lovely

63. The Wandsworth shield-boss showing the flowing circular designs of British La Tene in a specially fine example.

things, and the 'childish love of display' of which the classical writers spoke in describing the Celts. We find confirmation of those descriptions of the Celtic life-style by remarking on the kinds of object that were so lovingly and lavishly made and decorated: ceremonial war-gear, like the Battersea Shield, harness and chariot fittings like the Brentford cap, toilet articles, drinking vessels, and personal jewellery.

Hardly any evidence remains in Britain for the religious cults of the Celts. We know from written sources of the great power and prestige of the Druids, their priests. The Druids believed and taught the immortality of the soul, and the descent of all men from 'Dis Pater' a divine ancestor god. Dis Pater must be Dagda of Irish tradition, a powerful, club-swinging, cauldron-bearing warrior god, who is mated with various forms of earth-goddess. A number of such warlike, goddess-queens are recorded in Celtic belief, a confirmation of the high status of women among them, already suggested by the heroines of early Irish literature. Some of the little model animals found in Britain may be cult objects; of one god – Cernunnos – 'The Horned One' a couple of representations survive, and a settlement at Heathrow, in Middlesex contained a temple among its buildings. From Dagenham in Essex, from Ballachulish, Argyll, and Roos Carr, Yorks, there are wooden human figures, Celtic idols whose like was to be encountered centuries later by the first Christian missionaries.

The last comers to the British Isles before the Romans were a Celtic tribe called the Belgae, who were driven from their homelands in Gaul by the Romans, and the movements of Germanic tribes to the east of them. They came in large numbers as invaders, and rapidly took possession of most of south-eastern England. We know from the testimony of Julius Caesar that this invasion took place within a generation of his own time – that is around 75 BC. The Belgae brought with them the most efficient form of plough yet seen in Britain – an animal-drawn heavy plough with a coulter, designed to turn a sod, not merely to furrow the ground, as the lighter ploughs in use since the Bronze Age had done. They were therefore able to settle and cultivate the rich but heavy soils of the south-eastern valleys; the lack of archaeological finds of their farming settlements represents the continuous occupation and cultivation of those areas ever since.

As well as taking new land into cultivation, the Belgae brought into Britain the most well-organized society yet seen here. The Belgae established genuine urban settlements – the 'capitals' of their tribal chieftains. Although these towns were fortified with systems of dykes and ditches, they were quite different from the earlier hill-forts. Besides houses for the chief, his followers, craftsmen and traders they contained temples, workshops and shops; they were the administrative centres of wide areas, fulfilling all the functions of a modern town. These places, like Wheathampstead, or St Albans, or Colchester, were large enough to be called 'Oppida' – towns – by the Romans.

Belgic crafts were highly developed and skilled. They made wheel-thrown pottery on a large scale, turning out funeral urns, fine cups, platters and beakers, and many kinds of cooking and storage vessels. The town workshops also produced objects in bronze, including lathe-turned bowls, and fine work in late La Tene style, using gold enamel and shale as well as bronze, with undiminished talent and skill, as the famous Snettisham torque, from the territory of the Iceni in Norfolk amply demonstrates (see colour plate 14). Blacksmiths' work also reached a high level, and produced some fine things, like the splendid iron fire dogs, baskets and stands found as grave goods in burials (see plate 64).

The dead were cremated, and buried in cemeteries, and the class divisions in Belgic society show up clearly in the sharp distinction between poorly and richly furnished graves. Rich graves contained splendid objects, pottery, brooches, and buckets, adorned with bronze-work, like the Aylesford bucket (see plates 65, 66). Most lavish of all are the 'Vault' burials of the tribe of the Catuvellauni, which contain quantities of pottery, some imported, bronze vessels, wine-drinking equipment, and iron hearth fittings, accompanying cremated bones placed in a casket on or near a couch.

The Belgae were in close contact with Celtic tribes in Gaul from which they had come – indeed it was help for Gauls coming

64. One of a typical pair of Celtic iron fire dogs from Barton,
Cambridgeshire.

from across the English Channel, which provoked the Roman
invasion of Britain. They were within the orbit of influence of
Roman provincial society, and conducted a massive trade with
Rome and Gaul. Strabo gives us a list of goods that were exported
from Britain in the early first century AD – corn, livestock, metals,
leather, slaves, and hunting dogs. The export of slaves is graph-
ically illustrated by the grim object in plate 67. The imports
included quantities of pottery, drinking vessels, and wine.

A last striking demonstration of the social organization of the
Belgae is that they were the first inhabitants of Britain to use a

coinage. They must have brought the use of coinage with them from the continent, for finds of gold coins are among the earliest archaeological traces of their arrival, and their coins are based on Greek prototypes. Like the lovely coins they were modelled from, the Belgic gold coins are things of beauty (see colour plate 15). As the Roman influence grew, a silver and bronze coinage was added to the gold, and these later coins were often copies of Roman types.

65. Stave-built bucket with bronze mounts, from Aylesford, Kent.

66. The Aylesford Bucket.
Detail of handle mount with human head.

Latecomers as they were the Belgae had not spread beyond south-eastern Britain at the dawn of the Roman era; neither had the La Tène Celts before them entirely penetrated the remote and difficult terrain of the western and northern areas. The Iron Age of Scotland and Ireland is very different from that of the south-east. In the Western Isles, and the Highlands, the Iron Age farmsteads were round stone-built structures known as 'wheel-houses' – a glance at plate. 68 will show you why. The 'spokes'

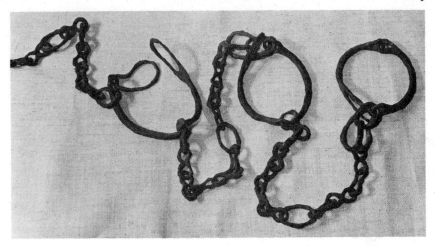

67. A Belgic slave-chain from Barton, Cambridgeshire.

were probably designed to help support the roof. Much stranger
are the chimney-like forts known as 'Brochs' with hollow, galler-
ied walls, that are found on the coasts (see plate 69). No one
knows against what danger they protected the northerners – slave
raids perhaps from the Belgic south, or from the Roman Empire.
But they are finely built, with double-skin walls, and staircases
in the thickness of the walls, and apparently date from the mid
first century B C. The people of the Brochs seem from their
pottery to have received refugees from southern Britain, and
perhaps also from France.

The Britain to which Julius Caesar came, therefore, was still
a melting pot, a mixed and disunited shifting amalgam of peoples.
In places a late Bronze Age way of life lingered on, changed very
little by making use of some iron; in the west and north a talented
and artistic La Tene culture, in touch on the seaways with the
Atlantic fringe of Europe, persisted, and was to persist, to form
one strand in Celtic Christendom when the Romans were long
gone; in the south and east a strong and successful group of
tribes were firmly if recently established, and determined to be
independent.

We know the name of the most powerful of the Belgic tribes

68. A 'Wheelhouse' at Sollas, North Uist.

– the Catuvellauni, and of their chieftain, Cassivellaunus, to whose leadership the tribes of Kent, attacked by Caesar, submitted themselves. We have therefore left the long dim prehistory of Britain, and entered upon its history. Cassivellaunus

69. The Broch of Mousa, Shetland.

was a barbarian lord – the leader of a society shaped by northern traditions, heroic, and uncivilized. He was confronted by the other European tradition, that of civilization, by the forces of urban, literate, classical antiquity. By a quirk of history it was in the person of one of the world's most famous men that the world of Rome came to that confrontation. But the men of Britain were not disgraced in the encounter.

Afterthought

Compared with the time covered in this book the time that lies between the present moment and Julius Caesar is tiny; and yet in that time nearly everything that determines the character of contemporary society, and the appearance of the landscape in Britain now has occurred. Nearly everything, but not quite all. Though everything has changed around them, the monuments of prehistoric times still remain. On open uplands, and in lonely places one can still see a landscape which, if not how prehistoric men found it, is still how they left it. We can still look at the things they made to wear, to farm and fight with, the landmarks they set upon the face of Britain to mark it for their own. And looking we may perhaps remember not only the gulf of time that divides us from those ancient makers, but the mysterious persistence in curious ways of ideas, techniques and images that teach us that we are their descendants still.

Looking at the White Horse of Uffington (see plate 70), for instance – a La Tene decoration made on chalk instead of bronze – we may wonder if it has some religious significance, and whether it connects with the British aversion to eating horsemeat. Or the stag mask of a Morris dancer may take our minds back to Star Carr. Perhaps staying in some place deep in the country we might hear how the blacksmith has been called out to drive iron nails in a path, to keep the ghosts from walking; and we might wonder if the magical powers attributed to iron and the men who work it go back to a time when iron was new and strange. I myself have seen an iron tyre laid red-hot round a wooden cartwheel, and the wheel with sparks flying bowled across the road like a child's hoop, to be dunked in a pool, in an explosion of steam, so that the iron shrank firmly on to the nearly charring wood – just so were the chariot wheels clad on which the Celtic warriors rolled to battle. Ploughing the Suffolk fields the farmer's boy will still turn up leaf-shaped blades of rippled flint in the furrows where some ancient hunter lost his arrowhead; I own one myself that lies beside me as I write; they were called 'elf-shot' before the Stone Age was dreamed of.

70. The White Horse of Uffington.

More than one ring of standing stones is called 'The dancing maidens' – is there some faint folk-memory of a ritual dance for which the ring was made? The midsummer sun still rises over the heelstone at Stonehenge. Towards Land's End a lacework of granite drystone walls marks on the land the tangled pattern of Iron Age fields.

Wherever we look in Britain the ancient past is all around us, and apt to come with us, unawares.

71. Stone circle on Cleator Moor, Cumberland.

APPENDIX I

🕸🕸🕸🕸🕸

Radiocarbon Dating and
the Tree-Ring Calibration

🕸🕸🕸🕸🕸🕸

RADIOCARBON dating has been available to archaeologists as an independent scientific check on their chronologies since shortly after the Second World War. Radiocarbon (also called carbon–14) is a rare variant form of carbon (a carbon isotope) produced in the atmosphere by the action of cosmic rays. It behaves exactly like ordinary carbon, combining chemically with oxygen to produce carbon dioxide, and in that form is distributed throughout the atmosphere. When plants take up carbon dioxide from the atmosphere they absorb some radiocarbon; when animals eat plants they absorb some radiocarbon, so that the carbon in the bodies of living things contains radiocarbon in the same tiny proportion as does the atmosphere.

Radiocarbon is radioactive. It very slowly 'decays' – that is it gives off an electron, and changes into nitrogen. The decay happens at a constant rate – half of any given amount of radiocarbon will have decayed in about 5,500 years. In another 5,500 years half of the remainder will have decayed – the original amount will have been reduced to one-quarter, and so on. This period of time is called 'The half-life' of radiocarbon.

The radiocarbon present in living tissue decays while the organism is still alive, but while it is still alive it is still taking up fresh radiocarbon, and the loss and gain balance out. But when the organism dies the radiocarbon is no longer renewed; the amount present at the moment of death begins to decay at the rate described above.

To date a sample of some once living thing – wood from an

DATE B.C. (calendar years)	BRITAIN	NORTH FRANCE	AEGEAN	BALKANS	EGYPT	DATE B.C. (calendar years)
1500						1500
2000	WESSEX Bronze	EARLY BRONZE AGE Bronze	Mycenae Shaft Graves MIDDLE BRONZE AGE	MIDDLE BRONZE AGE	MIDDLE KINGDOM	2000
	Stonehenge					
2500	BEAKER Copper Silbury Hill	BEAKER Copper	Phylakopi I Lerna (House of the Tiles) EARLY BRONZE AGE		EARLY DYNASTIC ← Bronze Hieroglyphs	2500
			Bronze Troy I Copper	Bronze		
3000	HENGES	LATE NEOLITHIC	EARLY BRONZE AGE	EARLY BRONZE AGE	PYRAMIDS	3000
	New Grange MEGALITHS CAUSEWAYED CAMPS and	LATER	FINAL	FINAL	Copper	
3500						3500
	LONG BARROWS	MEGALITHS	NEOLITHIC Occasional Copper	NEOLITHIC	PREDYNASTIC	
4000		PASSAGE GRAVES	Dhimini			4000
	FIRST FARMERS	FIRST FARMERS	MIDDLE	GUMELNITSA		
4500						4500
			NEOLITHIC	LATE VINČA Copper and Proto-writing		
5000						5000

Basic elements of the new chronology

archaeological site for example – one starts from the knowledge that in all living things there is the same small fixed proportion of radiocarbon, and measures how much of it is left. This allows one to calculate how much time has elapsed since the sample died.

The process involved is a great deal less simple than it sounds. The actual measurement is technically very difficult. This is because however old or young the sample may be the amount of radioactivity one is trying to measure is extremely small, much smaller than the background radiation always present from radioactive isotopes in materials in the laboratory, and from cosmic rays reaching the earth's surface while the measurement is taking place. Very elaborate steps have to be taken to cope with this difficulty, and the measurement is subject to a large margin of error; radiocarbon dates are given with an estimate of this margin of error – e.g. 3,590 BC + 130. This 'plus or minus' sign does not mean that the true date lies between 130 years before, and 130 years after the given date; it means that the true date has a $66\frac{2}{3}$ per cent probability of lying within that period; there is a calculable probability that it lies a small distance outside those limits, and a smaller probability that it lies far outside them. This degree of uncertainty arises from the difficulty of making accurate measurements; it does not take into account other possible sources of error, like 'contamination' of the sample by contact with newer or older sources of carbon while it lay in the ground, to name only one. Because of the limitations of the method, very little weight can be placed on one or two radiocarbon dates; but a pattern emerging from a whole set of datings is very strong evidence indeed.

When radiocarbon dates began to be published, during the fifties, the results surprised some archaeologists, and some even refused to accept them. They showed that farming was far more ancient than had formerly been supposed, for example. In Britain farming had begun, apparently, around 3,200 BC and not, as had formerly been supposed shortly after 2,000 BC. These results and others like them caused a good deal of controversy. And as research progressed it became apparent that the radiocarbon dates for early Egypt, and the calendar dates accepted by Egypt-ologists, and based on historical sources, did not agree as well as they should have done. In samples older than about 2,000 BC the radiocarbon levels were higher than expected, so that the sample was younger than would have been expected on the basis of archaeological knowledge. It seemed possible that the Egyptian historical dates were mistaken, though the grounds for accepting them were strong. The other possibility was that the amount of radiocarbon in the atmosphere had not, after all, always been exactly the same as it is today, but had varied in time, so that older samples having absorbed more radiocarbon than newer ones when they were alive, now appeared too young.

The proof that this latter possibility was indeed the case – that the amount of radiocarbon in the atmosphere had varied through time, and, even more important, some knowledge of when and by how much it had varied, came from a surprising source – from trees growing high in the White mountains of California. As you know, trees grow just under the bark, putting on an extra layer round the trunk in each calendar year. When a tree is cut down the layers show as rings on the stump, and by counting the rings you can find the age of the tree in calendar years. In 1955 some incredibly old trees – bristlecone pines – were found, the oldest of which had been alive for 4,900 years (taking us back to nearly 3,000 BC). Each tree-ring is of known date in calendar years; by taking a sample of one ring, and measuring the radiocarbon present in it, it became possible to check the scientists' prediction of how much radiocarbon ought to remain in a sample of that age. Tree-rings vary in thickness depending on the climatic con-ditions each year, and this fact has made it possible to match up rings from the early growth of one tree, with rings from other wood, and match the patterns of thick and thin rings. In this way it has been possible to piece together an overlapping sequence of tree-rings, which at present reaches back some 8,200 years.

The information gained from samples of tree-rings can then be used to work out a 'calibration' or correction that must be applied to radiocarbon measurements in calculating dates. The de-tails are very complex, because there have been many fluctuations in the amount of radiocarbon, and because not enough is known for certain about all the factors influencing the measurements. There is some suspicion, for example, that the tree-ring calibration slightly over-corrects radiocarbon dates. But broadly speaking the result is that radiocarbon dates before 1,200 BC must be set back several centuries. For dates around 3,000 BC the correction is as much as 800 years. The amount of radiocarbon present in the atmosphere, in short, was larger in 3,800 BC than it is now; things living then absorbed more of it, and thus have more of it left, and seem younger, than they would have done if the amount of radiocarbon had always been the same. When radiocarbon dates are corrected by the amounts suggested by the tree-rings the disagreement between them and the known Egyptian dates, which had been troublesome before, disappears, and they now agree very well.

But as we have seen, even uncorrected radiocarbon dates seemed very old to archaeologists when they were first published; the corrected ones really upset the applecart. They have the effect of making events in northern and western Europe much earlier by comparison with events in the Middle East and the Aegean basin than used to be supposed; and this has overthrown the accepted picture of European prehistory in the ways described in the text of this book, and others.

APPENDIX II

🔳🔳🔳🔳🔳

Indo-European Languages

🔳🔳🔳🔳🔳

WITH the exception of Basque, Finnish and Hungarian, all the languages now spoken in Europe, and America, and some of the languages of India, together with some extinct languages like Hittite and Tocharian can be shown to have so much in common that it is a reasonable guess that they are all descended from a single language spoken at some time in the distant past, and changing and breaking up into different languages as a result of the dispersal and wanderings of successive groups of people leaving the homelands of the language and scattering across the area where forms of the original language are now spoken.

All languages change with the passage of time; sometimes a mysterious change overtakes the pronunciation of a particular sound in all the words of a language; such a change is called a 'Sound Change'. Anybody who has learned more than one European language will have noticed certain similarities of form in words of the same or similar meaning. English acre, for instance, and Latin ager, a field. The words for mother and father, likewise, resemble each other in many languages. Careful comparison of Indo-European languages with each other makes possible the definition of sound changes which took place in the course of their divergence from each other. In the Germanic group of languages, for example, of which English is one, Indo-European 'b' became 'p' and Indo-European 'p' became 'f'. Knowing this we can see the resemblance between Latin la*b*or – I fall – and Old English sle*p*an – sleep – between Latin *p*edem – foot – and English-*f*oot which might otherwise escape notice.

There is no written Indo-European, nor are there written forms of the earliest languages that developed from it – of 'Common Germanic' for example, from which English, Dutch, German, Gothic and Norse, are descended. Nevertheless once careful comparison of words in the known Indo-European languages has allowed the sound changes in various groups of language to be described, it is possible to reconstruct the probable form of a word in Indo-European starting with the modern form and working the sound changes backwards. Such reconstructed forms are written with an asterisk in front of them to show that they are only guesses.

Let us take the English word COW as an example. It comes from the Old English word CU. There are similar words in other Germanic languages – KU in Old Frisian, KO in Old Saxon, KYR in Old Norse, etc. So we can reconstruct the Common Germanic word *KOUZ, fem. *KOZ. Such a word would have come from an Indo-European word *GWOUS. Now we can check up our guess by looking for the descendant of such a word, meaning cattle of some kind, in a language of another branch of the Indo-European family, in which different sound changes have occurred. We would find that Sanskrit has GAUS, and Greek has BOUS; Latin has BOS, BOVIS. (From which, by the way, French has BEOUF, from which Modern English gets BEEF. COW = BEEF!)

Take the word WHEEL as a second example. It comes from Old English HWEOL; and is equivalent to Old German WEL, Middle Dutch WIEL, Old Norse HJOL, etc. There must have been a Common Germanic word *XWEGULA – an Indo-European word *QᵂEQᵂLO. There is a Sanskrit word CAKRA meaning circle, a Greek word KUKLOS meaning cycle, a Latin word COLUS meaning a distaff (which spins round).

If a word, like wheel, occurs in all or many of the Indo-European languages, it is reasonable to suppose that it was a word of the original language; if the Indo-Europeans, whoever and whenever and wherever they were had a word for wheel, then it is reasonable to suppose that they had wheels to call by it. Laborious though it is, it is possible by sorting out which words

descend into all or most of the known Indo-European languages
to make a word-list of Indo-European vocabulary, and from the
vocabulary to extract information about the people who spoke it
and their homelands.

Indo-European has common words for birch, beech, oak, and
willow; for wolf, bear, goose, wasp and honey, salmon or a similar
large river fish. A belt of country north of the Black Sea, between
the Carpathian mountains and the Caucasus would fit very well;
so would the Danubian plain. The way of life implied by the
common vocabulary is that of farmers, growing cereals, and
keeping cattle, pigs, and sheep, and knowing horses, either wild
or domesticated. They knew one metal, which could have been
copper or bronze, and they were using wheeled transport of some
kind. We can also tell that they were a patriarchal society – words
for relations on the father's side are common to most language
groups, but words for maternal relatives are all different and so
must have been developed or borrowed by individual groups of
people after the dispersal. Some scholars think that certain institu-
tions, like the type of kingship, or the existence of council and
assembly, and methods of land-holding, should be regarded as
features of Indo-European culture, because forms of them are
very widespread among Indo-European speaking societies known
to us. On the one hand there could be other reasons for such
similarities of organization; on the other hand there are, for
example, startling similarities down to small details between Old
Irish Law-tracts, written down in the sixth or seventh centuries
AD and the Hindu Laws of Manu, at the opposite end of the
Indo-European world.

The identification of the Indo-Europeans with some particular
culture, in the archaeological record cannot be made with any
certainty. They might possibly be the users of pit graves and
hut graves in southern Russia around the middle of the third
millennium BC. Celtic is the earliest Indo-European language
which we can say with certainty was spoken in the British Isles;
but some scholars think they can detect in the river names of
north-western Europe, including Britain, a pre-Celtic, but still
Indo-European language. If they are right then one of the

incursions into the British Isles described in this book must have brought with it that lost Indo-European tongue. The Battle-axe people, coming from the assumed homelands of the Indo-Europeans, knowing the horse, using metal, warlike enough to be probably patriarchal, could possibly have been the ones.

🈓🈓🈓🈓🈓

BIBLIOGRAPHY

🈓🈓🈓🈓🈓

I   AUTHORITIES

Prehistory, Jaquetta Hawkes. George Allen and Unwin, 1963

A Background to Archaeology, D. Collins and others. Cambridge University Press, 1973

The Stone Age Hunters, Grahame Clark. Thames and Hudson, 1967; McGraw-Hill, New York, 1967

Pre-Roman Britain, Stanley Thomas. Studio Vista, 1965; New York Graphic Society, Greenwich, Connecticut, 1965

Archaeology by Experiment, John Coles. Hutchinson, 1973; Charles Scribner's Sons, New York, 1974

Prehistoric Art, T. G. E. Powell. Thames and Hudson, 1966; Praeger, New York, 1966

Palaeolithic Cave Art, Ucko and Rosenfeld. Weidenfeld and Nicolson: World University Library Series, 1967; McGraw-Hill, New York, 1967

Before Civilisation: The Radiocarbon Revolution and Prehistoric Europe, Colin Renfrew. Jonathan Cape, 1967; Alfred A. Knopf, New York, 1973

Prehistory, Derek Roe. Macmillan, 1970; University of California Press, Berkeley, 1970

Prehistoric Societies, Grahame Clark and Stuart Piggot. Hutchinson, 1965; Philadelphia Book Company, Philadelphia, 1965

Stonehenge, R. J. C. Atkinson. Hamish Hamilton, 1965

The Celtic Realms, Dillon and Chadwick. Weidenfeld and Nicolson, 1967

Everyday Life of the Pagan Celts, Ann Ross. Batsford, 1970

Everyday Life of the Pagan Celts, Ann Ross. Batsford, 1970; G. P. Putnam's Sons, New York, 1970

Etymology, Alan S. C. Ross. André Deutsch, 1958; British Book Centre, New York, 1958

Indo-European Origins: The Linguistic Evidence, A. R. Crossland. Past and Present 12: A Journal of Historical Studies, Past and Present Societies. Corpus Christi College, Oxford, 1957

2 FURTHER READING

(a) Non-Fiction:

Everyday Life in Prehistoric Times, M. and C. H. B. Quennell. Batsford, 1959;
 G. P. Putnam's Sons, New York, 1959
The Buildings of Ancient Man, Helen and Richard Leacroft. Brockhampton
 Press, 1973; Addison-Wesley, Reading, Massachusetts, 1973
Your Book of Prehistoric Britain, James Dyer. Faber and Faber, 1974
Collins Field Guide to Archaeology, Collins, 1963

(b) Fiction:

The Dream-Time, Henry Treece. Brockhampton Press, 1967; Hawthorn Books,
 New York, 1968
Warrior Scarlet, Rosemary Sutcliffe. Oxford University Press, 1958; Henry Z.
 Walck, New York, 1966
The Boy with the Bronze Axe, Kathleen Fidler. Chatto, Boyd and Oliver, 1968
The Stronghold, Mollie Hunter. Hamish Hamilton, 1974; Harper & Row,
 New York, 1974
Dom and Va, John Christopher. Hamish Hamilton, 1973; Macmillan, New
 York, 1973
Attar of the Ice Valley, Leonard Wibberley. Macdonald, 1969; Farrar, Straus &
 Giroux, New York, 1968
Throwstone of the Arctic, Sayles and Stevens. André Deutsch, 1962
Inheritors, William Golding. Faber and Faber, 1955; Harcourt Brace Jovanovich,
 New York, 1962
The Dawnstone, Jill Paton Walsh. Hamish Hamilton, 1973
Toolmaker, Jill Paton Walsh. Heinemann: Long Ago Children Series, 1974;
 Seabury Press, New York, 1974

INDEX